Eyes on the Skies: Area 51 Revealed

UFO Phenomena, Bob Lazar, De-Classified Documents

Created and Written by:

ORION LUMEN

TABLE OF CONTENTS

Introduction / Preface / Prologue

Chapter 1: Unveiling the Enigma of Area 51
Our journey begins at the epicenter of clandestine activities—
Area 51. Decades of secrecy have shrouded this remote military
base in Nevada, giving rise to a myriad of speculations.

Chapter 2: Roswell Revisited: A Legacy of Speculation
The Roswell incident, a cornerstone of UFO lore, beckons us to
revisit a moment in history when the skies seemingly played
host to extraterrestrial visitors. Unraveling the tangled web of
eyewitness accounts and government statements and
declassified materials that cast new light on this pivotal event.

Chapter 3: Unidentified Aerial Phenomena and the Global
Perspective
Beyond the borders of the United States, reports of unidentified
aerial phenomena have emerged from various corners of the
globe, declassified international documents and individual
testimonies, weaving together a narrative that transcends
national boundaries.

Chapter 4: Crop Circles and Cattle Mutilations: Earthly
Mysteries or Extraterrestrial Markers
Venturing beyond the realm of aerial encounters, we turn our
attention to the enigmatic phenomena of crop circles and cattle
mutilations. Through individual reports and declassified
studies, we explore the intricate patterns etched into fields and
the gruesome mysteries surrounding mutilated livestock.

Chapter 5: Bob Lazar and the Alien Technology Conundrum
At the heart of the UFO discourse lies the compelling testimony
of Bob Lazar, a whistleblower who claims to have worked on
reverse-engineering alien spacecraft at a location near Area 51.

Chapter 6: Military Encounters and Declassified Reports
From the annals of military history emerge encounters with
unidentified aerial phenomena, documented in declassified

reports from various branches of the U.S. military. We scrutinize these encounters, exploring the reactions of trained personnel to inexplicable aerial phenomena.

Chapter 7: Abduction Accounts: Personal Narratives and Classified Information
The phenomenon of alien abduction has long fascinated and terrified individuals who claim to have experienced otherworldly encounters. In this chapter, we examine both public and classified accounts of alien abductions, delving into the psychological and emotional aspects of these experiences.

Chapter 8: Atomic Level Engineering and Extraterrestrial Influence
As our understanding of physics and engineering advances, whispers of atomic-level engineering linked to extraterrestrial influence emerge. We explore declassified information and scientific speculations surrounding technologies purportedly beyond our current capabilities.

Chapter 9: International Collaboration on UFO Research:
Investigate how the declassification and sharing of UFO information have led to international collaboration on research and investigations. Explore the potential benefits and challenges of countries working together to understand these phenomena

Chapter 10: International Collaboration on UFO Research:
How the declassification and sharing of UFO information have led to international collaboration on research and investigations. Explore the potential benefits and challenges of countries working together to understand these phenomena.

Conclusion / Epilogue

Introduction:

In the shadowy realms of conspiracy theories and classified government projects, the UFO phenomena, Area 51, and the Roswell incident have long captured the imagination of the public. These enigmatic tales, once relegated to the fringes of speculation, have now found themselves thrust into the spotlight of public discourse. As governments around the world declassify long-guarded documents, a new era of transparency is emerging, unraveling the mysteries that have fueled decades of intrigue.

The very mention of Area 51 conjures images of clandestine activities, alien technology, and government secrecy. Meanwhile, the Roswell incident remains etched in history as the epicenter of UFO lore, sparking debates about extraterrestrial visitations and alleged cover-ups. The narrative surrounding these phenomena has not only permeated popular culture but has also given rise to a complex tapestry of public opinion, skepticism, and conspiracy theories.

Recent declassifications of documents related to unidentified aerial phenomena mark a paradigm shift. Governments are peeling back layers of secrecy, offering glimpses into encounters that were once dismissed or hidden. This newfound transparency invites us to reevaluate our understanding of aerial phenomena and question the boundaries of our knowledge about possible extraterrestrial technologies.

In weaving together the threads of Bob Lazar's revelations, military encounters, personal abduction accounts, and atomic-level engineering speculations, this exploration underscores the intricate interplay between classified information and public understanding. As the pages unfold, readers are invited to confront the enigma of the unknown, where government secrecy collides with personal narratives, reshaping our perception of what lies beyond the limits of conventional knowledge.

This book seeks to navigate the blurred lines between fact and speculation, exploring the impact of declassified documents on public perception. We delve into the challenges faced by those who dare to uncover the truth, the evolution of public opinion, and the ongoing quest for clarity in the face of mysterious encounters. As we sift through the pages of declassified information, we invite readers to contemplate the future trajectory of our understanding, poised on the brink of a new era in which the skies above may hold secrets yet to be fully revealed.

In the vast cosmic ballet, Earth's celestial companion, the moon, has long been shrouded in mystery, becoming a canvas for speculations about extraterrestrial phenomena and hidden structures. From whispered accounts of lunar bases to tantalizing hints of alien activity, the moon has captivated the imaginations of conspiracy theorists and cosmic enthusiasts alike. This deep dive delves into the accounts of lunar anomalies, exploring narratives of extraterrestrial bases, mysterious lights, and the intersection of cosmic curiosity with the unknown

Beyond lunar mysteries, accounts often extend to Earth's southernmost continent—Antarctica. Conspiracies intertwine lunar anomalies with tales of secret bases buried beneath the ice. The idea of extraterrestrial connections between the moon and Antarctica weaves a narrative where Earth's polar region becomes a terrestrial gateway to cosmic secrets. Though lacking empirical evidence, these accounts fuel the imaginations of those drawn to the cosmic unknown.

The exploration of extraterrestrial bases extends beyond the celestial to the terrestrial, with underwater bases entering the realm of speculative narratives. Stories emerge of submerged structures beneath Earth's oceans, often intertwined with lunar and Antarctic mysteries. The concept of cosmic gateways hidden beneath the waves serves as a bridge connecting lunar enigmas to Earth's unexplored aquatic depths.

As we navigate these accounts, it is crucial to distinguish between cosmic collaboration and conspiracy theories. While some narratives may be rooted in genuine curiosity and a quest for understanding, others border on the fantastical, intertwining lunar mysteries with tales of alien civilizations and covert government operations. Separating fact from fiction becomes a nuanced challenge in the cosmic landscape where imagination and reality dance in intricate choreography.

In analyzing and speculating on these unexplained phenomena and mysteries, one thread remains constant—the human quest for cosmic understanding. Whether grounded in scientific inquiry, fueled by conspiracy theories, or sparked by the allure of the unknown, our fascination with the moon's enigmas reflects the enduring human spirit to explore, question, and seek meaning in the cosmic expanse. The moon, once a symbol of mystery and wonder, continues to beckon us into the cosmic unknown, inviting us to unravel its secrets and redefine our place in the vastness of the celestial ballet.

Preface

In the vast tapestry of the unknown that shrouds our existence, certain enigmas stand as beacons, drawing humanity into realms where reality and speculation intertwine. Unidentified Flying Objects (UFOs) and Unidentified Aerial Phenomena (UAP) emerge as elusive threads in this cosmic mystery, sparking fascination, skepticism, and an insatiable curiosity about what lies beyond the confines of our terrestrial understanding.

This compilation delves into the realms of UFOs, UAP, and the accounts of whistleblowers, echoing the whispers of those who have stepped into the limelight, risking their own narratives against the backdrop of secrecy and skepticism. At the heart of this exploration is the testimony of individuals like Bob Lazar, whose revelations have reverberated through the corridors of conspiracy theories, government secrecy, and the ever-expanding cosmos of extraterrestrial possibilities.

As we embark on this journey, the intention is not to merely unravel the truth but to navigate the intricate landscapes of belief, skepticism, and the undeniable allure of the unknown. Each account, whether from the corridors of military installations or the quiet solitude of those who claim close encounters, adds a stitch to the fabric of speculation that envelops UFO phenomena.

The stories herein weave together firsthand experiences, government disclosures, and the tantalizing fragments of information that have emerged from the shadows of secrecy. From the classified corridors of Area 51 to the testimony of those who dare to defy official narratives, this compilation seeks to invite readers into the nebulous realms where reality and speculation dance in an intricate choreography.

However, as we embark on this journey, it is crucial to maintain a delicate balance between wonder and critical inquiry. The stories presented are fragments of a larger mosaic, and within them, we find a reflection of our collective yearning for understanding in the face of the cosmic unknown.

Let this compilation be a guide, not to definitive answers, but to the exploration of possibilities. The accounts within these pages are not offered as indisputable truths but as invitations to contemplate the mysteries that persist in the vast expanse of our cosmic existence. Whether one approaches these stories with skepticism, unwavering belief, or a curious blend of both, the goal remains the same—to inspire a dialogue that transcends the boundaries of conventional thought.

Prologue: A Cosmic Overture

In the grand theater of the cosmos, humanity stands at the brink of a new epoch—a chapter defined by the boundless reaches of space, the mysteries that adorn the celestial tapestry, and the collective yearning to unravel the enigmas that have captivated our imaginations for eons. This prologue serves as an overture, inviting you to envision a future where our endeavors to understand the cosmos converge with the audacious pursuits of establishing moon bases, colonizing Mars, and venturing beyond into the uncharted realms of our cosmic neighborhood.

As the Earth's denizens gaze skyward, a shared aspiration emerges—a yearning to transcend the boundaries of our home planet, to extend the reach of our collective human consciousness into the cosmos. The establishment of moon bases becomes a testament to our tenacity, a foothold on a celestial companion that has watched over us throughout the ages. It serves not only as a scientific outpost but as a symbol of our capacity to forge new frontiers, pushing the boundaries of what we once deemed impossible.

The dream to colonize Mars, our crimson neighbor in the night sky, echoes with the whispers of human ambition. In the Martian sands, we envision not only a new habitat for our species but a crucible for the evolution of our understanding, a laboratory where the sciences, arts, and humanities intermingle to shape a new chapter in the chronicles of our shared human story.

Beyond Mars, the call of the cosmos beckons, encouraging us to extend our gaze toward the distant stars. In our collective endeavors to reach farther, to touch the surfaces of distant planets, and perhaps one day stand witness to the birth of new worlds, we forge a legacy that transcends the confines of our terrestrial origins. It is a legacy not just of exploration but of understanding—a shared voyage into the cosmic unknown that unites us in a communion of human consciousness.

Let the stories that unfold within these pages serve as echoes of our aspirations. The exploration of UFOs, UAP, and whistleblower accounts becomes a thread woven into the grand tapestry of our cosmic endeavors. In the pursuit of understanding the mysteries that linger in the skies, we find a reflection of our ceaseless quest to expand our horizons, to push the boundaries of knowledge, and to embrace the awe-inspiring unknown.

I invite you to set sail on a celestial odyssey—one that transcends the limits of our terrestrial existence and propels us into a future where the stars are not just distant points of light but beacons guiding us toward a deeper understanding of who we are and what lies beyond. As we stand at the threshold of cosmic exploration, may the cosmic overture inspire a shared vision of humanity's communion with the cosmos, propelling us into a future where our collective consciousness expands like the universe itself— limitless, boundless, and filled with the promise of cosmic understanding.

As we seek truth and hope for a future of understanding our place in the universe and the fundamental questions of our existence, we navigate the realms of UFOs, UAP, and whistleblower accounts with an open mind, recognizing that the pursuit of truth is a journey, not a destination. In the shadowy landscapes of the cosmic unknown, may these accounts serve as lanterns, casting light on the paths that lead us deeper into the enigma of the uncharted and the unfathomable.

Remember, while the declassification of UFO documents is a significant development, it's crucial to approach these concepts with a discerning perspective, acknowledging the complexities of the phenomena and the various interpretations that may arise.

We will also delve into the first hand testimony accounts of Bob Lazar who worked at Area 51 in attempting to reverse-engineer a crashed alien spacecraft, as well as the following topics regarding UFOs and what is now called UAPs

1. Declassification of UFO Documents: Explore the recent trend of governments declassifying UFO-related documents, shedding light on previously undisclosed information. Investigate how this transparency impacts public perception and

contributes to the ongoing discussion on unidentified aerial phenomena.

2. Shift in Public Opinion: Examine how the release of UFO-related documents has influenced public opinion, fostering increased interest and belief in the possibility of extraterrestrial phenomena. Discuss the evolving societal attitudes towards UFOs and the implications for mainstream discourse.

3. International Collaboration on UFO Research: Investigate how the declassification and sharing of UFO information have led to international collaboration on research and investigations. Explore the potential benefits and challenges of countries working together to understand these phenomena.

4. Impact on National Security Policies: Analyze how the acknowledgment of UFO encounters affects national security policies. Explore whether there have been changes in how governments approach and respond to unidentified aerial phenomena, considering implications for defense strategies.

5. Scientific Community Engagement: Examine the involvement of the scientific community in analyzing declassified UFO data. Discuss how scientists contribute to the understanding of these phenomena and the challenges they face in studying unconventional aerial encounters.

6. Cultural and Media Influence: Explore the role of media and popular culture in shaping perceptions of UFOs, especially in the context of declassified documents. Discuss how these revelations are portrayed in movies, television, and other forms of entertainment.

7. Public Discourse and Conspiracy Theories: Analyze the impact of increased transparency on public discourse surrounding UFOs, considering how it may fuel both informed discussions and conspiracy theories. Examine the role of social media in shaping public narratives.

Weather you are a believer or a skeptic or accept that we have yet to fully understand what is behind these phenomena and government cover ups and classified documents, with an open mind we will look closely at what has been documented in an attempt to uncover the truth behind the what is considered to be the greatest mystery that continues to challenge our understanding of our own existence and place in the universe. Buckle up for a journey into Area 51 beyond the perimeters, eyewitness accounts of UFOs and alien abductions, and recently de-classified documents that shed light on possibilities of truth and the reality and nature of the extra terrestrial visitors to our planet.

Chapter 1: Unveiling the Enigma of AREA 51

In the vast expanse of the Nevada desert, concealed beneath the cloak of secrecy, lies the epicenter of clandestine activities—the notorious Area 51. As our journey unfolds, we are drawn into the enigma that has captured the collective imagination for decades.

The very mention of Area 51 conjures images of a hidden realm, a place where the veil between reality and speculation is thin. Nestled within the desolate landscape, this remote military base has been veiled in layers of secrecy, invoking curiosity, fascination, and a multitude of speculative tales.

Decades have passed since the first whispers of Area 51 reached the public consciousness. An aura of mystery envelopes this site, leaving us to ponder the nature of the activities transpiring within its heavily guarded confines. The landscape itself seems to be a silent witness to the clandestine affairs that have unfolded over time.

As declassified documents slowly emerge from the shadows, they offer a tantalizing glimpse into the secrets harbored by Area 51. Each revelation becomes a pixel in a mosaic of intrigue, painting a portrait of a place where reality blurs with the speculative. These documents, once tightly guarded, now beckon us to unravel the mysteries that have fueled decades of speculation.

Our exploration takes us beyond the classified labels and official denials, delving into the individual reports of those who claim to have ventured into the heart of Area 51. These firsthand accounts carry the weight of witness testimony, each narrative a piece of the intricate puzzle. The alleged sightings of unidentified aerial phenomena become brushstrokes on the canvas of the unknown, inviting us to consider the possibility of extraterrestrial encounters occurring within the confines of this secretive base.

Whispered accounts of reverse-engineering alien technology echo through the corridors of conspiracy theories. The very notion that within Area 51, scientists and engineers may be unraveling the secrets of extraterrestrial craft adds an element of science fiction to the narrative. These whispers, whether grounded in reality or speculative fiction, contribute to the mystique that surrounds this clandestine hub.

The complexity of the tapestry woven within Area 51 deepens as we navigate through these individual reports. Each account, tinged with intrigue and a sense of the unknown, adds layers to the narrative. The landscape, once barren and desolate, transforms into a canvas painted with the shades of secrecy, technological exploration, and the possibility of encounters beyond our earthly comprehension.

In the heart of Area 51, as declassified documents slowly come to light, our journey unveils not only the secrets held within its confines but also the enduring allure of the unknown. The stories, both whispered and documented, beckon us to contemplate the thin line between fact and fiction, reality and speculation. As we peel back the layers of secrecy, we find ourselves standing at the threshold of a realm where the mysteries of the extraterrestrial, the technological, and the clandestine converge.

Among the myriad tales that emerge from the shadows of Area 51, it is the first-hand accounts of those who claim to have stepped into the clandestine corridors that beckon us further into the heart of the mystery.

One such account comes from a former government engineer who, under the shroud of anonymity, detailed his experiences within the covert chambers of Area 51. He spoke of advanced technologies that defied the laws of physics as we understand them—craft that moved with an otherworldly grace, leaving seasoned engineers bewildered and in awe. His narrative, interwoven with technical jargon and a sense of reverence for the unknown, adds a layer of credibility to the speculation surrounding reverse-engineering endeavors.

Motivations behind the veil of secrecy, often attributed to the CIA and other government agencies, come into sharper focus through these firsthand accounts. National security becomes the driving force, an unyielding rationale for the classification of information. The specter of potential technological advancements falling into the wrong hands, whether foreign adversaries or entities with malicious intent, hovers over the decision to keep these mysteries concealed.

The narratives of those who have navigated the inscrutable landscapes of Area 51 highlight the palpable sense of duty that permeates these clandestine operations. Engineers and scientists, bound by oaths of secrecy, work diligently on projects that transcend the boundaries of conventional knowledge. The quest for technological superiority in the name of national security becomes both a moral imperative and a strategic necessity.

Yet, as we delve deeper into the motivations of government agencies, questions arise. Is the veil of secrecy solely driven by concerns about adversaries gaining access to groundbreaking technologies, or is there an element of preserving societal order in the face of paradigm-shifting revelations? The delicate balance between transparency and the preservation of stability becomes a central theme in understanding the motivations behind classified information.

As the narratives unfold, it becomes apparent that the mysteries enshrouding Area 51 are not solely about technological prowess. They are also about the delicate dance between the obligation to protect and the inherent human desire to explore the unknown. The motivations of the CIA and other government entities to keep these mysteries classified extend beyond the immediate concerns of national security; they delve into the intricate fabric of our collective consciousness.

In the murky depths of Area 51's classified endeavors, the stories of those who have borne witness illuminate the complexities of secrecy and the intertwined motivations that shape our understanding of the unknown. The narratives, both tantalizing and enigmatic, beckon us to contemplate the thin line walked by those who guard the secrets of our technological frontiers in the name of safeguarding a nation's well-being.

Speculation swirls like desert winds around the mysteries of Area 51, offering a kaleidoscope of possible explanations that range from the plausible to the fantastical. Among the myriad theories, some propose that the advanced technologies allegedly being developed within the base may be part of a classified space program, pushing the boundaries of propulsion and exploration beyond what is publicly known.

The whispers of reverse-engineering alien spacecraft fuel another strand of speculation, suggesting that within the sealed chambers of Area 51, scientists are attempting to decipher the secrets of extraterrestrial technology. Whether grounded in reality or veering into the realms of science fiction, this theory captivates the imagination and adds a layer of intrigue to the secretive operations within the base.

Conspiracy theories, often intertwined with government secrecy, posit that Area 51 conceals evidence of past extraterrestrial encounters, and perhaps even ongoing communication with alien civilizations. Some propose that the technology being developed is not just ahead of its time but sourced from interactions with beings from other worlds.

The veil of secrecy, according to another line of speculation, may also hide experimental aircraft and surveillance technologies designed to monitor global adversaries. This perspective views Area 51 as a crucible of innovation, where the defense industry collaborates with government agencies to maintain a strategic advantage in an ever-evolving geopolitical landscape.

As we navigate these speculative currents, questions arise about the motivations behind the secrecy. Could it be that the revelations within Area 51 extend beyond the realm of extraterrestrial technology to encompass experimental psychological operations or mind-bending research that challenges our understanding of consciousness itself?

The mysteries might also be rooted in more mundane explanations, such as the development of advanced weaponry or unmanned aerial vehicles. In this scenario, the secrecy would be aimed at maintaining a technological edge in conventional warfare, aligning with the prevailing narrative of national security.

Ultimately, the true nature of the mysteries concealed within Area 51 remains elusive, obscured by layers of classification, government denials, and the enduring allure of the unknown. The base's enigma persists as a testament to the complex dance between secrecy and revelation, where each theory, no matter how speculative, adds another brushstroke to the intricate canvas of speculation that shrouds this clandestine hub.

Chapter 2: Roswell Revisited: A Legacy of Speculation

The Roswell incident, a cornerstone of UFO lore, beckons us to revisit a moment in history when the skies seemingly played host to extraterrestrial visitors. Unraveling the tangled web of eyewitness accounts and government statements, we delve into declassified materials that cast new light on this pivotal event. Amidst the enduring debate over weather balloons and crashed saucers, we examine how public opinion has shifted in the wake of declassification and what this means for our collective understanding of potential extraterrestrial contact.

The Roswell incident, an enduring enigma in the tapestry of UFO lore, invites us to journey back to a fateful moment in history when the New Mexican skies became the stage for a cosmic drama. The narrative, forever etched into the annals of extraterrestrial speculation, revolves around the purported crash of a mysterious object, triggering a legacy of speculation that resonates to this day.

As we embark on this intellectual odyssey, the very air becomes charged with the intrigue surrounding Roswell. Eyewitness accounts, like fragments of a puzzle, form the initial threads of our exploration. Testimonies of locals who stumbled upon debris and anomalous materials intertwine with tales of unearthly beings, creating a narrative woven with both awe and uncertainty. The human imagination, fueled by the mysterious nature of the recovered artifacts, has given rise to a myriad of theories that transcend the boundaries of conventional understanding.

Decades after the incident, declassified materials emerge as beacons of illumination, shedding fresh light on the Roswell saga. As the cloak of government secrecy is lifted, a nuanced understanding of the events begins to take shape. We scrutinize once-classified documents that hint at military operations, weather experiments, and top-secret projects in the vicinity, challenging the prevailing narrative of extraterrestrial visitation.

The enduring debate over the nature of the crashed object, oscillating between weather balloons and extraterrestrial spacecraft, becomes a central point of contention. The revelation that the military initially confirmed the crash of a "flying disc" only to retract the statement and attribute it to a weather balloon adds layers of complexity to the Roswell narrative. We find ourselves caught in a web of conflicting accounts, where the distinction between truth and obfuscation blurs, leaving us to navigate the uncertainties that linger over the New Mexican desert.

Public opinion, a dynamic force that ebbs and flows like the tides, emerges as a critical element in the Roswell saga. In the wake of declassification, a seismic shift occurs in the collective perception of the incident. Where once there was steadfast belief in extraterrestrial contact, skepticism takes root as alternative explanations gain traction. The Roswell incident becomes emblematic of the broader struggle between official narratives and public skepticism, shaping the landscape of UFO discourse for generations to come.

As we delve deeper into this complex narrative, the legacy of Roswell takes on new dimensions. It becomes a reflection of societal trust, the power dynamics between citizens and authorities, and the persistent allure of the unknown. Roswell, once a mere blip on the historical radar, evolves into a symbol of our collective fascination with the possibility of extraterrestrial life and the elusive quest for truth.

The Roswell incident, revisited through the lens of declassified materials and evolving public opinion, transcends its status as a mere historical event. It becomes a microcosm of our eternal quest for answers in the face of mysteries that defy easy explanation. The legacy of Roswell persists not only as a chapter in the UFO chronicles but as a timeless exploration of the human psyche and our unyielding curiosity about the cosmos.

As we peer deeper into the heart of the Roswell incident, the shadows of secrecy loom larger, casting an ominous silhouette over the narrative. This clandestine veil, thickened by the complexities of the Cold War era, extends beyond Roswell to the epicenter of UFO lore—Area 51. The strict rules governing access to this enigmatic base create an impenetrable barrier, giving rise to legends and fueling the speculation that swirls around its classified operations.

Area 51, nestled within the unforgiving terrain of the Nevada desert, operates under a cloak of extreme secrecy. The stringent rules governing access to this military installation have become legendary, creating an aura of mystery that transcends its physical boundaries. Trespassing into the restricted zone is met with swift and severe consequences, invoking the full force of legal measures designed to deter the curious and protect the classified nature of the operations within.

The roots of this secrecy trace back to the Cold War, an era when geopolitical tensions and the race for technological superiority were at their zenith. Area 51 emerged as a crucible for cutting-edge aviation technology and clandestine operations, shielded from the prying eyes of both domestic and foreign entities. The strict rules governing access were forged in this crucible, becoming an integral component of a complex web of national security measures.

The whispers of extraterrestrial technology, reverse engineering, and experimental aircraft fueled by classified projects imbue Area 51 with an air of mystique. The need for absolute secrecy is perceived not merely as a desire for privacy but as an imperative to safeguard technological advancements that could tip the scales of global power. The strict rules, enforced with military precision, are a testament to the gravity of the secrets harbored within.

The public's fascination with Area 51's secrecy amplifies its allure. The mere mention of the base evokes visions of hidden hangars, advanced aircraft, and technologies that defy conventional understanding. The rules governing access contribute to the mystique, fostering an environment where speculation and conspiracy theories flourish. Area 51 becomes a symbol of the lengths to which governments will go to protect their technological edge.

The strict rules surrounding Area 51 also contribute to the enduring legacy of UFO lore. The perceived connection between the base and extraterrestrial phenomena elevates its status in the collective imagination. The limited information available, coupled with the strict enforcement of access rules, creates a void that is filled by speculation, giving rise to a narrative where the forbidden nature of Area 51 becomes inseparable from its legendary status.

The strict rules governing access to Area 51 form an integral part of its mystique and the broader tapestry of UFO lore. Shrouded in secrecy, this military installation becomes a symbol of the delicate balance between national security imperatives and the public's insatiable curiosity. As we navigate the shadows cast by classified operations, the rules that govern access to Area 51 underscore the enduring allure of the unknown and the complexities of maintaining secrecy in an era where information is both power and currency.

As we delve deeper into the mysteries of Area 51, the echoes of nuclear testing reverberate through its history, leaving a seismic imprint on the landscape. The clandestine base, initially established as a test site for high-altitude reconnaissance aircraft during the Cold War, evolved into a hub for covert military operations, including the testing of nuclear weaponry.

The historical context of nuclear testing in Area 51 is integral to understanding its transformation. In the aftermath of World War II, the United States entered into a nuclear arms race with the Soviet Union. The need for secure and secluded locations to test atomic weapons became paramount. Area 51, with its vast and desolate expanse, offered the ideal setting for these classified experiments.

Etched into the geology of the Nevada Test and Training Range, which encompasses Area 51, is the ground bears witness to the detonation of countless nuclear devices, leaving behind craters, scorched earth, and a haunting legacy of the destructive power unleashed during these experiments. Classified tests, such as Operation Ranger and Operation Greenhouse, underscore the critical role played by Area 51 in advancing the U.S. nuclear arsenal.

Beneath the surface of this seemingly barren landscape lies a labyrinth of underground structures, adding another layer to the mystique of Area 51. These subterranean facilities, shielded from prying eyes, became essential components of the base's evolution. The need for secrecy and protection from potential Soviet reconnaissance drove the construction of extensive underground complexes.

The underground structures of Area 51 are rumored to house cutting-edge laboratories, testing facilities, and storage areas for classified projects. Speculation abounds regarding the nature of these facilities, with theories ranging from advanced aircraft development to the purported reverse engineering of extraterrestrial technology. The secrecy surrounding these underground chambers fosters an environment where rumors and legends intertwine with the tangible evidence of covert operations.

The development of advanced aircraft, such as the iconic U-2 and the stealthy SR-71 Blackbird, was closely linked to the subterranean laboratories of Area

51. These aircraft, born from the crucible of classified research, redefined the boundaries of aviation technology and played pivotal roles in intelligence gathering during the Cold War. The hangars and testing grounds hidden beneath the desert floor became crucibles of innovation, where engineers pushed the limits of what was technologically possible.

The subterranean world of Area 51, coupled with the evidence of nuclear testing, transforms the base into a living testament to the complexities of Cold War military endeavors. The scars of atomic detonations and the hidden chambers beneath the earth's surface bear witness to the marriage of innovation and secrecy, creating an enduring legacy that transcends its historical confines.

The evidence of nuclear testing and the underground structures of Area 51 intertwine to form a narrative that stretches beyond the confines of conventional military history. As we navigate the complex web of classified experiments and hidden facilities, we uncover a tapestry woven with threads of technological innovation, geopolitical tension, and the enduring quest for secrecy in the face of global uncertainties. Area 51 stands not just as a symbol of clandestine military operations but as a living testament to the transformative power of the unknown.

Delving further into the Roswell incident, we confront the persistent specter of potential cover-ups and the intricate dance between official explanations and the demands of an inquisitive public. The narrative's evolution intertwines with the complexities of the Cold War era, where secrecy and the race for technological supremacy cast a long shadow over the quest for truth.

The weather balloon explanation, initially proffered by the military, becomes a focal point in unraveling the layers of the Roswell mystery. Official statements asserting the recovery of a weather balloon and its associated radar target calibration devices offer a rational, albeit mundane, explanation. However, skepticism emerges as inconsistencies in the narratives surface. How could a weather balloon, a common piece of equipment, generate such fervor and secrecy? The incongruities between eyewitness testimonies of unearthly debris and the official account trigger a palpable sense of skepticism, challenging the veracity of the weather balloon explanation.

The demand for truth, a rallying cry that echoes through the years, becomes an integral part of the Roswell legacy. The public's insatiable appetite for answers intensifies as new generations seek clarity on a pivotal moment in UFO history. The emergence of grassroots movements and advocacy for government transparency propels the demand for a reexamination of the Roswell incident. The rallying cry of "Truth about Roswell" becomes emblematic of a collective yearning for disclosure.

Conspiracy theories, often born from the fertile ground of mistrust, take root as alternative explanations gain momentum. The notion that the weather balloon account is a smokescreen for a more elaborate cover-up gains traction. The Roswell incident transforms into a symbol of the struggle between governmental authority and the right of citizens to access information that may reshape their understanding of the world.

The intricacies of Cold War geopolitics cast a long shadow over Roswell, adding layers of complexity to the narrative. The fear of the unknown, amplified by the nuclear arms race and geopolitical tensions, provides a backdrop against which government secrecy finds fertile ground. The potential existence of classified military projects and experimental technology further muddies the waters, creating a space where speculation flourishes.

In the face of these uncertainties, the demand for truth regarding Roswell becomes a potent force. Citizen-led initiatives, investigative journalism, and persistent questioning of official narratives shape the ongoing quest for transparency. The legacy of Roswell is not merely a historical footnote but an ongoing dialogue between those who hold the keys to classified information and a public clamoring for a fuller understanding of the events that unfolded in the New Mexican desert.

The Roswell incident stands as a nexus of historical intrigue, public demand for truth, and the complexities of Cold War secrecy. The interplay between cover-up speculations, weather balloon explanations, and the unwavering demand for transparency forms a multifaceted narrative that transcends its historical confines. Roswell becomes a timeless symbol of the intricate relationship between those who govern and those who seek to unravel the mysteries that shape our collective consciousness.

Chapter 3: Unidentified Aerial Phenomena and the Global Perspective

Beyond the borders of the United States, reports of unidentified aerial phenomena have emerged from various corners of the globe. This chapter explores declassified international documents and individual testimonies, weaving together a narrative that transcends national boundaries. As governments cooperate in sharing information, we consider the implications of a globalized effort to comprehend the mysteries that hover above us.

In the vast expanse of our global skies, a symphony of unidentified aerial phenomena (UAP) unfolds, transcending national borders and capturing the collective curiosity of nations. As we venture beyond the confines of the United States, this chapter embarks on a journey into the realms of declassified international documents and individual testimonies, seeking to unravel the mysteries that hover above us.

The narrative takes flight against the backdrop of a world interconnected by both technological advancements and shared glimpses of the unknown. Governments worldwide grapple with reports of UAP, and declassified documents offer a rare glimpse into the collaborative efforts to understand these enigmatic phenomena. This globalized perspective shifts our gaze from the confines of national boundaries to a collective endeavor fueled by the shared pursuit of knowledge.

International cooperation in sharing information about UAP reflects a departure from the historical hesitancy to disclose such encounters. Governments, once guarded about acknowledging sightings, now engage in a delicate dance of transparency. The declassification of documents becomes a thread woven into the fabric of a new era, where nations recognize the need to pool resources and knowledge in the face of aerial mysteries that defy conventional understanding.

As we navigate through declassified international documents, patterns emerge that echo the multifaceted nature of UAP encounters. Sightings range from fleeting glimpses by military personnel to more sustained observations by civilians, creating a tapestry of experiences that traverse cultural, linguistic, and geopolitical divides. The implications of this globalized effort extend beyond mere acknowledgment; they delve into the heart of humanity's shared quest for comprehension in the face of the extraordinary.

Individual testimonies, irrespective of nationality, contribute threads to this intricate narrative. Pilots, astronomers, and everyday citizens share accounts that resonate across borders, challenging preconceived notions about the nature of our skies. The democratization of information, facilitated by the interconnected world we inhabit, amplifies the impact of these personal narratives, fostering a sense of shared wonder and uncertainty.

The collaborative pursuit of understanding UAP reframes the narrative surrounding these phenomena. No longer confined to the realm of speculative folklore, the globalized effort transforms the conversation into one informed by diverse perspectives, scientific rigor, and a collective yearning for answers. The challenges posed by UAP, once considered isolated incidents, now draw upon the combined expertise of nations as they grapple with the complexities of unidentified aerial encounters.

We start to see a panorama of global perspectives on unidentified aerial phenomena. The declassified documents and individual testimonies transcend borders, inviting us to contemplate the interconnected nature of our shared skies. As governments navigate the delicate balance between disclosure and secrecy, the globalized effort to comprehend the mysteries above us becomes a testament to our collective journey into the uncharted realms of the extraordinary.

As we embark on a deep dive into the world of unidentified aerial phenomena (UAP), the pages of declassified reports and individual accounts unfurl before us, revealing a tapestry woven with intrigue, uncertainty, and the uncharted territories of our shared skies. These relevant reports and accounts transcend geographic boundaries, offering glimpses into encounters that have captivated the attention of governments and citizens alike.

One of the key documents that emerges from the vaults of international intelligence agencies is the "Cometa Report," a French initiative that explored the UAP phenomenon comprehensively. Declassified in 1999, this report stands as a landmark in acknowledging the reality of unidentified aerial phenomena and calling for a collaborative, global effort to understand these encounters. Its findings, drawn from military and civilian sources, underscore the need for increased scientific attention to the phenomena.

In parallel, the United Kingdom's Ministry of Defence (MOD) released a trove of declassified documents known as the "UFO files." Spanning several decades, these files document thousands of sightings, investigations, and correspondences with the public. While many sightings were attributed to conventional explanations, a significant number remained unexplained, fostering a sense of mystery that echoed beyond British borders. The transparency exhibited by the UK MOD sets a precedent for governmental openness about UAP encounters.

Australasia contributes its own piece to the puzzle with New Zealand's "The Project Blue Book." Declassified in the early 1980s, this report details the investigations conducted by the Royal New Zealand Air Force into UAP sightings. It provides a glimpse into how a smaller nation grappled with the challenges posed by unidentified aerial phenomena and the efforts to maintain a balance between secrecy and public awareness.

Individual accounts, ranging from military personnel to civilians, weave through the declassified reports, adding a human dimension to the UAP narrative. A notable example is the testimony of retired U.S. Navy pilot David Fravor, whose encounter with a mysterious, fast-moving object off the coast of California in 2004 garnered widespread attention. Fravor's detailed account, supported by radar data and corroborating witnesses, exemplifies the complexities inherent in UAP encounters.

Civilian reports also echo from across the globe. From the hills of Brazil to the deserts of Australia, individuals from diverse walks of life have documented their experiences with unexplained aerial phenomena. These accounts, often submitted to governmental agencies or shared through civilian-led initiatives, amplify the kaleidoscope of perspectives that contribute to our understanding of the unknown.

The globalized nature of UAP encounters becomes evident when examining reports from military collaboration, such as the North Atlantic Treaty Organization's (NATO) records. Documents declassified by NATO shed light on incidents involving military aircraft encountering UAP and the subsequent efforts to analyze and understand these occurrences. The cooperative sharing of information among member nations underscores the gravity of these encounters in the realm of international security.

As we navigate through these reports and accounts, recurring themes emerge. The persistent challenges faced by investigators include the elusive nature of UAP, the potential technological advancements exhibited by these objects, and the delicate balance between public disclosure and national security imperatives. The reports collectively paint a picture of an evolving understanding, where governments grapple with the complexities of unidentified aerial phenomena in an interconnected world.

The deep dive into relevant reports and accounts surrounding UAP offers a panoramic view of encounters that transcend borders. From government-initiated investigations to individual testimonies, the collective narrative unfolds as a testament to the shared mystery of our skies. The globalized effort to comprehend unidentified aerial phenomena stands at the intersection of science, diplomacy, and the enduring human quest to unravel the enigmatic forces that dance above us.

As we plunge into the depths of unidentified aerial phenomena (UAP), a complex tapestry of details and speculations unfurls, inviting us to navigate the intricacies of encounters that defy conventional understanding. These phenomena, reported across the globe, span decades and traverse the realms of military investigations, government disclosures, and individual testimonies. The details encapsulated within declassified reports and personal accounts form a mosaic that tantalizes the imagination, while speculations hover on the precipice between scientific inquiry and the unexplored territories of the extraordinary.

One of the intriguing details that emerges from declassified reports is the recurring theme of accelerated technological capabilities exhibited by UAP. Witnesses, including trained military personnel and seasoned pilots, describe objects that defy the known laws of physics, executing maneuvers beyond the capabilities of earthly aircraft. The sheer speed, agility, and abrupt changes in direction displayed by these unidentified objects challenge the limits of human understanding. Speculation arises not only about the origin of such technology but also about the potential implications for our understanding of propulsion systems and aerodynamics.

Speculations also weave through the labyrinth of encounters documented in international reports, such as the Cometa Report in France. This comprehensive investigation acknowledges the reality of UAP and speculates on the extraterrestrial hypothesis. The idea that these phenomena may originate from civilizations beyond our planet adds a layer of speculation that transcends national borders. The question of whether humanity is witnessing the presence of advanced extraterrestrial intelligence becomes a tantalizing aspect of the UAP narrative, with the Cometa Report sparking a renewed discussion on the potential cosmic origins of these enigmatic encounters.

Within the realm of declassified reports, another intriguing detail emerges—the consistent challenge faced by military and intelligence agencies in categorizing and explaining UAP encounters. The term "unidentified" itself underscores the difficulty in ascribing conventional explanations to these phenomena. While some sightings may eventually be attributed to natural phenomena, weather balloons, or experimental aircraft, a substantial number remain unexplained. Speculation swirls around the persistent gap in our understanding, leading to questions about whether there are truly unknown and potentially otherworldly elements at play in the skies above.

Individual testimonies, such as those from military personnel like David Fravor, contribute rich details to the UAP narrative. Fravor's encounter with a fast-moving object off the coast of California in 2004 provides vivid descriptions of an anomalous craft that seemed to defy the laws of physics.

The personal nature of these accounts adds a human dimension to the speculation surrounding UAP. Questions about the psychological and emotional impact on those who bear witness to the unknown become integral to the broader conversation, highlighting the profound implications of encounters that transcend the realm of ordinary experience.

The globalized effort to understand UAP, reflected in international collaboration and the sharing of information, introduces a fascinating detail—the convergence of perspectives from diverse cultures and geopolitical contexts. Governments, once guarded about acknowledging these encounters, are increasingly open to collaborative investigations. Speculation arises about whether a shared understanding of UAP could lead to a new era of global cooperation in the exploration of the unknown. The potential for a unified effort to decipher the mysteries above us becomes a tantalizing prospect, fueled by the collective curiosity of humanity.

As we navigate through these details and speculations, a central theme emerges—the persistent dance between the known and the unknown. The details, whether gleaned from declassified reports or individual accounts, paint a picture of encounters that defy easy categorization.

Speculations, ranging from extraterrestrial visitation to advanced human technology, orbit the fundamental question of what lies at the core of the UAP phenomenon. The exploration of these mysteries becomes not only a scientific endeavor but a philosophical and existential journey that challenges the boundaries of human knowledge.

The deep dive into the details and speculations surrounding unidentified aerial phenomena invites us into a realm where the ordinary meets the extraordinary. Whether examining the technological feats displayed by UAP, contemplating the cosmic origins of these encounters, or grappling with the psychological impact on witnesses, we find ourselves at the nexus of curiosity and uncertainty. The intersection of details and speculations propels us into a frontier where the boundaries of the known dissolve, leaving us to ponder the profound implications of the mysteries that hover above us.

Chapter 4: Crop Circles and Cattle Mutilations: Earthly Mysteries or Extraterrestrial Markers

In the mosaic of unexplained phenomena that dots our terrestrial landscape, the enigmatic occurrences of crop circles and cattle mutilations stand as beguiling puzzles, captivating the collective imagination. As we delve into the annals of historical accounts and sift through the tapestry of evidence, the narrative unfurls a complex dance between genuine mysteries and the shadowy realm of hoaxes and deception.

Crop Circles: Intricate Patterns in the Fields

Crop circles, those geometric marvels etched into fields of wheat and corn, have long eluded a concrete explanation. Reports of these intricate formations date back centuries, with anecdotes describing mysterious circles appearing overnight. The complexity of some patterns defies the notion of human origin, sparking debates about the involvement of extraterrestrial intelligence. However, within the intricate labyrinth of crop circles, a parallel narrative emerges—one tainted by the brushstrokes of human artistry.

The historical roots of crop circles trace back to pre-modern times, with references to circular patterns found in folklore and ancient writings. However, the modern era witnessed a surge in reported occurrences, particularly in the late 20th century. The patterns evolved from simple circles to elaborate designs, captivating the public and spawning a subculture of enthusiasts who sought to unravel their mysteries. The allure of the unknown propelled researchers into fields, cameras in hand, capturing the intricate beauty that adorned the landscape.

Decades of speculation prompted scientific investigations into the nature of crop circles. Declassified studies reveal a spectrum of explanations, from natural phenomena like whirlwinds to human-made creations using planks and ropes. While some patterns remain unexplained, the overarching conclusion tends to lean toward terrestrial origins. Yet, the allure of extraterrestrial involvement persists, fueled by the intricate beauty and the lingering question: could all crop circles be mere human artistry?

As we shift our focus to the unsettling mysteries of cattle mutilations, the landscape transforms into a tableau of macabre occurrences. Reports of livestock found with precision-cut incisions and organs removed without a trace evoke a sense of dread and fascination. The phenomenon extends beyond mere folklore, with documented cases raising questions about the perpetrators and their motivations.

Individual reports of cattle mutilations read like chapters from a horror novel. Witnesses describe finding livestock with surgical precision, blood drained, and organs excised with eerie accuracy. The gruesome scenes spark fear and speculation, with fingers pointing in various directions—from extraterrestrial entities conducting experiments to clandestine government operations seeking to study the effects of radiation on animal tissue. The narrative twists and turns, leaving a trail of unanswered questions and a lingering unease in rural communities.

Faked Accounts: The Dark Side of Mystery

Amidst the genuine mysteries of crop circles and cattle mutilations, the specter of human deception casts a shadow over the landscape. Hoaxes, fueled by a desire for attention or perpetuated by pranksters, muddy the waters of investigation. Crop circles crafted with planks and rope, and cattle mutilations staged for dubious reasons, blur the line between the authentic and the fabricated. The pursuit of truth becomes a delicate dance, where distinguishing the genuine from the contrived requires meticulous scrutiny.

As we try to make sense of the labyrinth of crop circles and cattle mutilations, the journey unfolds as a convergence of wonder and skepticism. The intricate patterns in the fields and the gruesome scenes in pastures invite us to contemplate the mysteries that linger at the intersection of the known and the unknown.

While historical accounts and declassified studies shed light on earthly origins, the shadow of faked accounts looms, reminding us of the complexity inherent in unraveling terrestrial enigmas. The dance between truth and deception continues, urging us to peer into the depths of these mysteries with a discerning eye, recognizing that within the tapestry of crop circles and cattle mutilations, the genuine and the fabricated coalesce in a dance as enigmatic as the phenomena themselves.

As we plunge deeper into the enigmatic world of crop circles, the narrative unfolds with intricacies that challenge simplistic explanations. The origins of these mysterious patterns, some so elaborate and precisely arranged that human artistry seems inadequate, beckon us to explore the possibility of cosmic origins.

Possible Origins: Natural Forces and Extraterrestrial Artistry

Declassified studies and scientific investigations have explored various explanations for crop circles, ranging from natural phenomena like whirlwinds to human-made hoaxes. However, the complexity of certain formations resists easy categorization. The intricate designs that seemingly defy the capabilities of human creators raise questions about the potential involvement of extraterrestrial intelligence. Some argue that the precision and mathematical complexity of these formations hint at a cosmic origin beyond our current understanding.

Intricate Designs: Mathematical Symmetry and Sacred Geometry

Crop circles are not mere random patterns; they often exhibit mathematical symmetry and sacred geometry. Elaborate designs, resembling fractals and geometric shapes, evoke a sense of cosmic artistry. The precision with which crops are bent, not broken, suggests a deliberate and intricate process. Some formations mirror ancient symbols and archetypal imagery, leading enthusiasts and researchers to ponder the possibility of a universal language communicated through these agricultural canvases.

Nature of Crops: Burned and Bent in Cosmic Choreography

One of the perplexing aspects of genuine crop circles lies in the nature of the crops themselves. In authentic formations, the crops are often not only bent but display characteristics that challenge conventional explanations. Nodes in the plant stems are sometimes expanded or altered in a way that suggests exposure to an external force. Moreover, in some instances, the crops exhibit a form of "scorching" or burning that defies the mechanisms of human-made crop circle hoaxes. These peculiarities deepen the mystery, prompting further speculation about the involvement of unknown forces.

The meanings behind crop circles remain an elusive enigma. Speculation abounds regarding whether these intricate designs serve as a form of cosmic communication, a message from extraterrestrial intelligences attempting to convey information to humanity. Some enthusiasts interpret the symbols as messages of peace, unity, or warnings about the state of our planet. Others view crop circles as Earth's response to cosmic energies or as expressions of consciousness encoded in the very fabric of the crops.

The exploration of crop circles transcends the confines of human-made hoaxes. The possibility of natural forces, extraterrestrial artistry, and the intricate designs that challenge our understanding of geometry and plant physiology propel the narrative into the realm of cosmic wonder. As we unravel the meanings woven into the fields, the dance between terrestrial tapestry and cosmic communication invites us to peer into the depths of possibility.

The crop circles, whether created by unknown cosmic forces or the hands of artistic extraterrestrial entities, remain a canvas upon which the mysteries of our existence are painted, challenging us to decode the patterns and symbols that grace the Earth's agricultural landscapes.

Chapter 5: Bob Lazar and the Alien Technology Conundrum

At the heart of the UFO discourse lies the compelling testimony of Bob Lazar, a whistleblower who claims to have worked on reverse-engineering alien spacecraft at a location near Area 51. We delve into Lazar's detailed accounts of the spacecraft's interior, the challenges posed by its advanced technology, and the radiation dangers he described. As we examine the controversies surrounding Lazar's claims, we navigate the intersection of classified information, personal narratives, and the enduring mystery of extraterrestrial technology.

In the labyrinthine corridors of UFO lore, few figures cast a shadow as intriguing and controversial as Bob Lazar. At the nucleus of the discourse surrounding unidentified aerial phenomena and extraterrestrial technology, Lazar's testimony unfolds as a riveting narrative that challenges conventional understanding. As we embark on a deep dive into Lazar's claims, we navigate the intricacies of his detailed accounts of reverse-engineering alien spacecraft, the enigmatic interior of these otherworldly vessels, the technological challenges they posed, and the haunting specter of radiation dangers. At this crossroads of classified information, personal narratives, and the persistent allure of extraterrestrial mysteries, we find ourselves on a journey into the heart of the alien technology conundrum.

Lazar's narrative begins with assertions that he worked at a location near Area 51, known as S-4, where he claims to have engaged in reverse-engineering activities on extraterrestrial spacecraft. His detailed accounts provide a glimpse into the interior of these advanced vehicles, describing the propulsion systems, the layout of the control room, and the peculiarities of the materials used. The richness of Lazar's descriptions amplifies the speculative fervor surrounding the notion that humanity may have stumbled upon technology not of terrestrial origin.

Some of the most fascinating descriptions we here from Bob Lazar include:

1. Interior of Alien Spacecraft: Explore Bob Lazar's detailed descriptions of the interior of the alleged alien spacecraft, focusing on the unique features he claimed to have encountered. Discuss how his

accounts have influenced popular perceptions of extraterrestrial technology.

2. Radiation Dangers and Technological Challenges: Investigate Lazar's claims about the dangers of radiation associated with the alien technology he worked on. Delve into the technological challenges he described in trying to understand and replicate the advanced propulsion systems of the spacecraft.

3. Materials and Propulsion Systems: Examine Lazar's insights into the materials purportedly used in the construction of the spacecraft and the unconventional propulsion systems. Explore how these details have sparked discussions within the scientific and ufology communities.

4. Verification Challenges and Skepticism: Discuss the challenges faced in verifying Lazar's claims, including the lack of tangible evidence and the skepticism from various quarters. Explore how this skepticism has shaped public perceptions and the credibility of his narrative.

5. Government Response and Denials: Analyze the official responses and denials from the government regarding Lazar's claims. Explore the dynamics between whistleblowers, government secrecy, and the efforts to debunk or dismiss the allegations.

6. Cultural Impact of Lazar's Revelations: Examine how Bob Lazar's disclosures have influenced popular culture, including their portrayal in media, literature, and discussions within the UFO and conspiracy theory communities. Consider the lasting impact of his story on the broader narrative of extraterrestrial encounters.

7. Scientific Perspectives on Lazar's Claims: Explore how scientists and experts have reacted to Lazar's assertions, analyzing the scientific feasibility of the technologies he described and whether any of his claims align with known principles of physics and engineering.

Remember, while Bob Lazar's story has captured public interest, it's important to approach these concepts with a critical mindset, acknowledging the lack of concrete evidence and the controversial nature of his claims.

As we delve into Lazar's intricate accounts of the spacecraft's interior, we encounter a technological landscape that defies our understanding of physics. Advanced propulsion systems, based on the manipulation of gravity waves, challenge the very principles that govern conventional aeronautics. The alleged existence of an element with atomic properties beyond those found on Earth, specifically Element 115, becomes a linchpin in Lazar's narrative. Speculation arises not only about the feasibility of such technologies but also about the implications for our understanding of the cosmos and the potential for interstellar travel.

The challenges posed by the advanced technology Lazar describes become a focal point in our exploration. From the complexities of harnessing gravitational forces to the utilization of Element 115 as a potential fuel source, the alleged capabilities of these spacecraft stretch the boundaries of known science. The speculative landscape expands as we contemplate the implications of mastering technologies that could revolutionize our approach to energy, propulsion, and the exploration of the cosmos. The intersection of imagination and scientific inquiry blurs as we ponder the tantalizing prospect of unlocking the secrets hidden within the alleged extraterrestrial blueprints.

Yet, woven into the fabric of Lazar's narrative are warnings of radiation dangers associated with the alien technology. The potential perils of interacting with these advanced systems, including the risks of exposure to exotic materials, introduce an element of caution to the fantastical narrative. Speculation arises about the ethical and safety considerations that would accompany the possession and study of extraterrestrial technology. The haunting specter of unforeseen consequences, whether in the form of health risks or unintended technological repercussions, adds complexity to the already enigmatic landscape.

Controversy envelops Lazar's claims, with skeptics questioning the authenticity of his background and the veracity of his accounts. The absence of tangible evidence, coupled with inconsistencies in his narrative and difficulties in corroborating his employment history, fuels skepticism within the UFO community and beyond. Speculation emerges not only about the potential government cover-up of extraterrestrial technology but also about the motivations and credibility of those who step forward as whistleblowers in the realm of classified information.

As we navigate through the controversies surrounding Lazar's claims, the intersection of classified information, personal narratives, and the enduring mystery of extraterrestrial technology becomes a focal point. The tension between the desire for transparency and the imperative of national security underscores the challenges inherent in navigating the complex landscape of UFO disclosures. Speculation arises not only about the veracity of individual claims but also about the broader implications for our understanding of the cosmos, the potential for technological advancements, and the delicate dance between revelation and secrecy.

The deep dive into Bob Lazar's testimony unveils a narrative that exists at the crossroads of the extraordinary and the skeptical. The richness of his descriptions, the technological intricacies he details, and the controversies surrounding his claims propel us into a realm where speculation and inquiry converge. As we grapple with the alien technology conundrum, we find ourselves navigating the delicate interplay between personal narratives, the quest for truth, and the enduring allure of the mysteries that lie beyond the limits of our known reality.

In the annals of UFO lore, Bob Lazar's detailed descriptions of the interior of the alleged alien spacecraft stand as a cornerstone, shaping and challenging popular perceptions of extraterrestrial technology. Lazar's accounts, born from his claimed experiences at S-4 near Area 51, paint a vivid picture of an otherworldly environment with unique features that defy our understanding of engineering and physics. As we embark on a deep dive into Lazar's descriptions, we navigate the contours of the alleged extraterrestrial interiors, explore the technological nuances he purportedly encountered, and grapple with the speculative implications for our perception of advanced civilizations beyond our planet.

Lazar's narrative unfolds within the confines of a control room that defies the conventions of earthly technology. He describes a scene where gravity amplifiers, rather than traditional propulsion systems, dictate the movement of the spacecraft. The control panels, according to Lazar, lack conventional buttons or switches, relying instead on a form of tactile manipulation that responds to the touch of the operator. The absence of familiar interfaces challenges the very foundations of our understanding of human-machine interaction, speculating on the potential for advanced cognitive interfaces that transcend our current technological landscape.

The alleged presence of an "Element 115" becomes a linchpin in Lazar's descriptions, shaping the technological landscape of the spacecraft's interior. He contends that this element, not naturally occurring on Earth, serves as a crucial component for the advanced propulsion system. The speculation surrounding Element 115 extends beyond Lazar's accounts, becoming a focal point in the broader discourse on potential extraterrestrial technologies. The existence of such an element would redefine our understanding of materials science and introduce new possibilities for energy generation and propulsion.

The interior of the alien spacecraft, as described by Lazar, also encompasses an unconventional power source. Instead of relying on traditional fuel, the propulsion system purportedly taps into the inherent gravitational forces of the craft. The manipulation of gravity waves as a means of travel challenges our understanding of physics and opens avenues for speculation about advanced civilizations harnessing fundamental forces of the universe. The implications of such technology extend beyond propulsion, raising questions about the potential for manipulating gravity for other practical applications.

The layout of the control room, according to Lazar, reflects an ergonomic design that adapts to the physiology of the extraterrestrial occupants. Seats with integral limb supports and accommodations for beings with different anatomies suggest a level of customization that transcends human-centric design principles. Speculation arises about the adaptability of advanced civilizations to diverse environments and the potential for technology to seamlessly integrate with the unique characteristics of extraterrestrial life forms.

These detailed descriptions, while captivating, exist within a landscape fraught with controversy and skepticism. The absence of tangible evidence, coupled with challenges in corroborating Lazar's employment history, has led many to question the authenticity of his accounts. Skepticism intersects with the popular imagination, creating a dichotomy where some view Lazar as a whistleblower unveiling the secrets of advanced technology, while others dismiss his claims as unfounded or even fabricated.

The influence of Lazar's accounts on popular perceptions of extraterrestrial technology cannot be understated. His detailed descriptions, whether embraced or scrutinized, have permeated popular culture, shaping depictions of alien spacecraft in media, literature, and discussions about UFOs. The iconic image of a saucer-shaped craft powered by unconventional technology, derived from Lazar's testimony, has become ingrained in the collective consciousness of those fascinated by the mysteries of the cosmos.

Bob Lazar's detailed descriptions of the interior of the alleged alien spacecraft transcend the realm of personal narratives, weaving into the fabric of our cultural understanding of extraterrestrial technology. The unique features he claims to have encountered challenge and captivate the popular imagination, influencing how we perceive the potential capabilities of advanced civilizations. As we navigate the speculative landscape carved by Lazar's accounts, we find ourselves at the nexus of fascination, skepticism, and the enduring quest to unravel the enigmatic technologies that may exist beyond the boundaries of our known reality.

Bob Lazar's accounts of radiation dangers associated with the alleged extraterrestrial technology and the technological challenges he described in understanding and replicating the advanced propulsion systems of the spacecraft are pivotal elements in the intricate tapestry of UFO lore. As we embark on a deep dive into Lazar's narrative, we navigate the complexities of his assertions, scrutinize the potential implications of radiation exposure, and delve into the formidable obstacles encountered in deciphering the mysteries of propulsion systems that defy the limits of our current scientific understanding.

Lazar contends that the alien spacecraft he claimed to have worked on utilized an exotic material known as Element 115 as a crucial component in its propulsion system. According to his accounts, this element served as a fuel source, facilitating the manipulation of gravity waves for propulsion. However, the extraction and utilization of Element 115 posed profound technological challenges. Lazar described the intricate process of introducing the element into the reactor and the subsequent generation of gravitational waves. The ability to harness and control these waves presented a formidable obstacle, as the technology involved was unlike anything within the realm of terrestrial science.

The challenges Lazar described in understanding and replicating the advanced propulsion systems extended beyond the realm of theoretical physics. He asserted that the gravity amplifiers used in the spacecraft's propulsion system operated on principles fundamentally different from known aeronautical engineering. Traditional propulsion mechanisms, such as jet or rocket engines, rely on the expulsion of mass to generate thrust. In contrast, the alleged alien technology harnessed the manipulation of gravitational forces, ushering in a paradigm shift that defied conventional wisdom.

The technological challenges inherent in deciphering the propulsion systems were compounded by the alleged adaptability of the craft's control mechanisms. Lazar described a tactile interface devoid of conventional switches or buttons, where operators manipulated the craft through a touch-based system. This unconventional mode of control added layers of complexity to the understanding of human-machine interaction, challenging researchers to conceive of interfaces that transcended the limitations of conventional engineering.

However, amid these technological challenges, Lazar introduced a sobering element into the narrative—the dangers of radiation associated with alien technology. He described encountering a mysterious substance within the propulsion system that emitted harmful radiation. The potential risks posed by exposure to this exotic material became a central concern, shaping both the operational procedures within the alleged S-4 facility and the broader implications for those tasked with studying and replicating the extraterrestrial technology.

The radiation dangers Lazar described introduced an ethical dimension to the exploration of advanced extraterrestrial technology. The potential health risks associated with exposure to unknown materials raised questions about the ethical responsibilities of those engaged in classified research. Speculation arose not only about the physiological effects of the alleged radiation but also about the broader implications for the safety and well-being of individuals tasked with unraveling the mysteries of the extraterrestrial craft.

Skeptics and critics have questioned the authenticity of Lazar's claims, pointing to inconsistencies in his narrative and difficulties in verifying his employment history. The absence of tangible evidence and the classified nature of the work he purportedly engaged in have fueled skepticism within the UFO community and the broader scientific community. The challenges of corroborating Lazar's accounts have contributed to the ongoing debate surrounding the veracity of his assertions and the potential for a government cover-up of advanced extraterrestrial technology.

The exploration of Bob Lazar's claims about radiation dangers and technological challenges associated with alleged extraterrestrial technology invites us into a realm where scientific inquiry intersects with ethical considerations and the mysteries of the cosmos. The technological hurdles Lazar described, from the utilization of exotic materials to the manipulation of gravitational forces, challenge our understanding of propulsion systems.

The specter of radiation dangers adds a dimension of caution to the pursuit of extraterrestrial knowledge, raising ethical questions about the responsibility of those engaged in the exploration of technologies that may exist beyond the boundaries of our known reality. As we navigate this complex landscape, the intersection of technological intrigue, ethical considerations, and skepticism forms a nexus where the quest for truth unfolds against the backdrop of the enduring enigma of unidentified aerial phenomena.

The official responses and denials from the government regarding Bob Lazar's claims represent a complex interplay between whistleblowers, government secrecy, and concerted efforts to debunk or dismiss the allegations. Lazar's assertions, centered around his alleged experiences at S-4 near Area 51, have prompted reactions ranging from outright denial to nuanced statements that neither confirm nor refute the specifics of his accounts. As we delve into the dynamics of government responses, we navigate the landscape of secrecy, skepticism, and the challenges inherent in discerning truth amid classified operations.

From the outset, government agencies, including the United States Air Force and the Department of Defense, issued categorical denials of Lazar's claims. Officials refuted the existence of S-4 and dismissed Lazar's purported employment there. These denials, often characterized by brevity and a lack of detailed explanations, sought to distance the government from the allegations, portraying Lazar's narrative as baseless and without merit. The strategy of outright denial aimed to quell public curiosity and mitigate the potential fallout from the explosive nature of the claims.

The broader context of government secrecy, particularly concerning classified military operations and facilities, adds a layer of complexity to the official responses. The veil of secrecy shrouding Area 51 and related installations contributes to an environment where the government is reluctant to provide detailed information, even in the face of sensational claims. The inherent tension between transparency and national security imperatives underscores the challenges in disentangling fact from fiction within the realm of classified operations.

Whistleblowers like Lazar, who come forward with allegations of clandestine activities, often face a formidable wall of skepticism and scrutiny. The government's historical track record of debunking or discrediting whistleblowers contributes to a climate where public trust in such revelations is inherently strained. Efforts to paint whistleblowers as unreliable or motivated by personal agendas serve to undermine their credibility and dissuade others from coming forward.

In Lazar's case, the government response included efforts to scrutinize his background and cast doubt on his qualifications and employment history. Skeptics pointed to discrepancies in Lazar's educational and professional record, suggesting that he embellished his credentials or fabricated aspects of his story. The focus on discrediting the whistleblower himself rather than addressing the substance of his claims is a common tactic employed to diminish the impact of potentially damaging revelations.

The government's approach to addressing Lazar's claims extends beyond denials and skepticism to active efforts to control the narrative. Through the careful curation of information and the selective release of details, officials seek to shape public perception and maintain control over the discourse surrounding classified projects. The strategic dissemination of information, often through authorized channels, allows the government to assert authority and project an image of stability, even in the face of controversial allegations.

Decades after Lazar first came forward, the government's stance has evolved from outright denial to a more nuanced acknowledgment of the existence of Area 51. While officials have confirmed the presence of the base, they remain reticent about the details of specific projects or operations conducted there. This shift in approach reflects a delicate balance between acknowledging certain aspects of classified activities and preserving the broader veil of secrecy.

The ongoing secrecy surrounding classified military installations perpetuates an environment where the veracity of claims like Lazar's remains challenging to ascertain conclusively. The classification of information, justified on grounds of national security, serves as both a shield and a sword in the government's response. While it provides a rationale for withholding details and issuing denials, it also contributes to a narrative of suspicion and intrigue that fuels public fascination with the unknown.

The government's responses and denials regarding Bob Lazar's claims embody a multifaceted strategy that includes outright rejection, efforts to discredit the whistleblower, and controlled information dissemination. The dynamics between whistleblowers, government secrecy, and the efforts to debunk or dismiss allegations underscore the complexities inherent in navigating the intersection of classified operations and public disclosure. As the enigma of Area 51 and related installations persists, the quest for transparency and understanding remains entangled with the enduring challenges posed by the clandestine world of government activities.

Bob Lazar's revelations have left an indelible mark on popular culture, permeating various mediums such as media, literature, and discussions within the UFO and conspiracy theory communities. His claims, centered around extraterrestrial technology and government secrecy, have become a cultural touchstone that continues to captivate the collective imagination. As we delve into the cultural impact of Lazar's disclosures, we navigate the ways in which his narrative has shaped depictions of UFOs, influenced public perceptions of government activities, and contributed to the enduring fascination with the mysteries of the cosmos.

One of the primary avenues through which Lazar's revelations have reverberated in popular culture is the media. His story has been featured in documentaries, television programs, and interviews, each contributing to the dissemination of his claims to a broader audience. The iconic image of saucer-shaped spacecraft and the alleged technologies described by Lazar have become emblematic of the UFO narrative. Media representations often oscillate between presenting Lazar as a credible whistleblower and portraying his accounts as part of a larger landscape of conspiracy theories. This dual portrayal adds layers of complexity to the cultural reception of his revelations, allowing for interpretations that span from awe to skepticism.

Literature has also been influenced by Lazar's disclosures, with his story serving as inspiration for fictional narratives exploring the intersection of extraterrestrial encounters and government secrecy. Science fiction novels and speculative literature draw on the themes introduced by Lazar, weaving tales that imagine the consequences of advanced alien technologies falling into human hands. The blurred line between fiction and reality within these literary works contributes to the enduring allure of Lazar's narrative, embedding it within the broader tapestry of speculative storytelling.

Within the UFO and conspiracy theory communities, Lazar's disclosures have sparked extensive discussions and debates. Online forums, social media platforms, and dedicated conferences provide spaces for enthusiasts and skeptics alike to dissect the details of his claims. The enduring popularity of Lazar's story within these communities reflects a broader cultural fascination with government secrecy, extraterrestrial encounters, and the pursuit of hidden truths. The discourse within these circles often involves not only the veracity of Lazar's specific claims but also the broader implications for our understanding of the cosmos and the potential existence of advanced extraterrestrial civilizations.

Lazar's impact on popular culture extends beyond his initial disclosures, permeating broader discussions about government transparency and the existence of unidentified aerial phenomena. The narrative he introduced has become a reference point for subsequent revelations and discussions surrounding classified military projects. The themes of secrecy, whistleblowing, and the quest for truth resonate with broader cultural anxieties about the reach of government power and the potential existence of technologies beyond the public's awareness.

The portrayal of Lazar's story in popular culture has contributed to the shaping of archetypes within the UFO narrative. He embodies the figure of the whistleblower, an individual who, at great personal risk, steps forward to unveil hidden truths. This archetype resonates with broader cultural narratives of resistance against powerful institutions, adding a layer of heroism to Lazar's role within the UFO discourse. Simultaneously, the skepticism and controversies surrounding his claims serve as cautionary tales about the challenges of navigating the terrain between secrecy and revelation.

The lasting impact of Lazar's revelations lies in their ability to fuel ongoing discussions about the existence of extraterrestrial life, the reach of government secrecy, and the boundaries of human knowledge. His narrative has become a cultural touchstone that continues to shape how we perceive the unknown and the lengths to which institutions may go to conceal certain truths. The enduring fascination with Lazar's story underscores the cultural significance of narratives that challenge established paradigms and invite individuals to question the official accounts of reality.

Bob Lazar's disclosures have become woven into the fabric of popular culture, influencing depictions of UFOs, inspiring literary works, and sparking discussions within communities dedicated to exploring the unknown. His impact extends beyond the specifics of his claims, resonating with broader cultural themes of secrecy, resistance, and the pursuit of hidden truths. As the cultural narrative of extraterrestrial encounters continues to evolve, Lazar's story remains a cultural touchstone that invites individuals to contemplate the mysteries that lie beyond the boundaries of our everyday understanding.

Chapter 6: Military Encounters and Declassified Reports

From the annals of military history emerge encounters with unidentified aerial phenomena, documented in declassified reports from various branches of the U.S. military. We scrutinize these encounters, exploring the reactions of trained personnel to inexplicable aerial phenomena. The declassification of military documents sheds light on how governments handle such incidents and the impact these encounters have on national security policies.

In the vast landscape of military encounters with unidentified aerial phenomena (UAP), declassified reports offer a portal into a realm where trained personnel grapple with the inexplicable. As we embark on a deep dive into these encounters, the narratives woven within declassified military documents unveil the reactions of servicemen and women facing the unknown skies. The process of declassification itself becomes a lens through which we explore how governments handle such incidents, the implications for national security policies, and the speculative tendrils that extend into the enigmatic nature of these encounters.

Declassified military reports often serve as glimpses into moments where the ordinary collides with the extraordinary. Witnessed by trained and disciplined personnel, these encounters carry a weight of credibility that distinguishes them from civilian reports. The narratives unfold in the terse language of military documentation, providing a stark contrast to the sensationalism often associated with UFO discussions. The very act of declassification suggests a willingness to share previously guarded information, opening a window into a dimension where the military grapples with the limits of its understanding.

The reactions of military personnel to UAP encounters range from awe to trepidation, revealing a spectrum of emotions and responses that transcend the typical narratives of skepticism or disbelief. Trained observers, including pilots and radar operators, articulate the challenges they face in reconciling the observed phenomena with conventional explanations. The stark juxtaposition between the structured world of military training and the chaotic dance of unexplained aerial objects introduces a psychological dimension to the encounters, leaving an indelible mark on those who bear witness.

Declassified reports also illuminate the intricate dance between the desire for transparency and the imperative of national security. The act of declassification implies a strategic decision to reveal information previously withheld from public view. This process raises questions about the motivations behind the disclosure—whether driven by a genuine commitment to openness, a calculated effort to manage public perceptions, or a recognition of the need to address the growing wave of public interest in UAP. The declassification of military documents becomes a narrative in itself, shaping the public discourse surrounding military encounters with the unknown.

The impact of UAP encounters on national security policies becomes a focal point of exploration within declassified reports. Governments, tasked with safeguarding the interests of their nations, grapple with the implications of aerial phenomena that defy easy classification. The potential for advanced technologies or unconventional threats prompts military and intelligence agencies to reassess their strategic postures. Speculation arises not only about the technological capabilities displayed by UAP but also about the strategic implications for defense and geopolitical stability. The intersection of military encounters and national security policies introduces a layer of complexity that extends beyond the immediate awe-inspiring nature of the phenomena.

Speculation also weaves through the narratives found within declassified reports. The tantalizing details of unexplained aerial objects executing maneuvers beyond the capabilities of known aircraft invite conjecture about the origins and intentions behind these phenomena. The notion of extraterrestrial visitation becomes a whispered undercurrent in discussions surrounding military encounters, fueled by the inability to attribute observed behaviors to conventional human technology. The speculative landscape extends beyond earthly explanations, embracing the possibility that these encounters may represent interactions with civilizations beyond our planet.

As we navigate through the depths of declassified military reports, the narratives within these documents become fragments of a larger mosaic that challenges our understanding of the unknown. The act of declassification, while shedding light on specific incidents, also raises broader questions about the nature of government disclosure, the complexities of national security, and the perpetual dance between revelation and secrecy. The speculative tendrils that intertwine with these narratives invite us to contemplate not only the encounters themselves but also the broader implications for our perception of the cosmos and the place of humanity within the vast expanse of the unknown.

The deep dive into military encounters with unidentified aerial phenomena, documented in declassified reports, invites us into a realm where the disciplined world of the military collides with the inexplicable. The reactions of trained personnel, the process of declassification, and the implications for national security policies paint a nuanced picture of encounters that transcend the boundaries of the ordinary. As we navigate through the speculative currents that weave through these narratives, we find ourselves on a journey into the enigmatic, where the disciplined gaze of the military meets the mysteries that hover beyond the edge of our understanding.

Recently declassified reports have thrust into the public eye encounters involving Tic Tac-shaped objects, witnessed by Air Force pilots. These incidents, documented with increasing frequency, depict unexplained aerial phenomena that defy the known laws of physics. As we delve into these reports, the mysterious propulsion systems displayed by these Tic Tac-shaped objects become a focal point, challenging our understanding of aerospace capabilities and opening speculative gateways into realms beyond the limits of conventional physics.

The Tic Tac encounters, often described by seasoned pilots as objects exhibiting extraordinary maneuverability, raise fundamental questions about the propulsion mechanisms propelling these enigmatic craft. Declassified reports detail instances where these objects display acceleration and deceleration rates that surpass the capabilities of any known human-made aircraft. The absence of visible means of propulsion, such as exhaust plumes or traditional propulsion systems, adds to the mystique surrounding the nature of these unidentified craft.

The propulsion systems observed in these encounters defy conventional understanding, prompting speculation about technologies that operate on principles currently beyond the grasp of terrestrial engineering. Witness accounts describe seamless transitions between extreme velocities and sudden stops, maneuvers that challenge the very foundations of aerodynamics as we know them. The question of how these objects achieve such feats becomes a puzzle that transcends the boundaries of known physics.

The absence of observable propulsion methods, coupled with the unconventional movements exhibited by the Tic Tac-shaped objects, introduces the possibility of propulsion systems based on principles beyond our current comprehension. Speculation arises about the potential harnessing of exotic physics, gravitational manipulation, or propulsion systems that operate in dimensions beyond the conventional three spatial dimensions. The speculative landscape expands to contemplate technologies that may be rooted in advanced scientific principles, pushing the boundaries of what we understand about the nature of propulsion.

These encounters, documented in declassified reports, fuel discussions about the potential origins and capabilities of the Tic Tac-shaped objects. The elusive nature of these craft, combined with their ability to perform maneuvers inconsistent with known aircraft, prompts questions about whether they represent classified human-made technologies, extraterrestrial visitations, or phenomena that challenge our understanding of reality. The enigma surrounding the propulsion systems of these objects adds layers of complexity to the ongoing debate within scientific and military communities.

As we navigate the recently declassified reports, the propulsion systems displayed by the Tic Tac-shaped objects invite us to contemplate the intersection of cutting-edge technology, advanced physics, and the mysteries that pervade our skies. The documentation of these encounters, previously shielded from public view, initiates a dialogue not only about the immediate implications for national security but also about the broader implications for our understanding of the universe. The speculative pathways carved by these reports extend into uncharted territories of scientific inquiry, challenging us to reevaluate our preconceptions about the nature of propulsion and the possibilities that may lie beyond the boundaries of our current scientific understanding.

the recently declassified reports of Tic Tac-shaped objects encountered by Air Force pilots open a portal into a realm where the propulsion systems displayed defy the known laws of physics. The absence of conventional propulsion methods and the extraordinary maneuvers witnessed in these encounters raise profound questions about the nature of these unidentified aerial phenomena. As we grapple with the mysteries embedded in these reports, we find ourselves on a journey into uncharted scientific territories, contemplating the tantalizing prospect that the propulsion systems of these enigmatic craft may operate on principles that challenge the very fabric of our understanding of the cosmos.

Chapter 7: Abduction Accounts: Personal Narratives and Classified Information

The phenomenon of alien abduction has long fascinated and terrified individuals who claim to have experienced otherworldly encounters. In this chapter, we examine both public and classified accounts of alien abductions, delving into the psychological and emotional aspects of these experiences. As declassified information intertwines with personal narratives, we navigate the complex terrain of subjective encounters with the unknown.

The intricate and haunting phenomenon of alien abductions is truely a realm where personal narratives intertwine with classified information, inviting us to navigate the complex terrain of subjective encounters with the unknown. As we embark on this deep dive, we unravel the psychological and emotional dimensions of abduction accounts, exploring both public disclosures and the shadowy realm where classified information intersects with the deeply personal stories of those who claim to have experienced otherworldly encounters.

Public accounts of alien abductions form a tapestry of experiences that range from terrifying to transcendent. Individuals who come forward with these narratives often describe encounters with non-human entities, recounting episodes of being taken against their will, subjected to medical examinations, and returned with fragmented memories. The psychological toll of these experiences is palpable, as abductees grapple with the challenge of reconciling extraordinary memories with the skepticism and disbelief they often encounter from the broader society.

Decades of reports and personal testimonies have given rise to common themes within abduction narratives. The presence of otherworldly beings with distinct characteristics, such as large eyes and slight frames, echoes across diverse accounts. The use of advanced medical procedures, often involving reproductive examinations, becomes a recurring motif, generating speculation about the potential motives and interests of these alleged extraterrestrial entities. The psychological trauma inflicted on abductees by these encounters adds an emotional layer that transcends the boundaries of the purely scientific or rational.

In the shadowy corridors of classified information, a parallel narrative unfolds. Whistleblowers and individuals claiming insider knowledge have hinted at the existence of secret government programs dedicated to studying and understanding alien abduction phenomena. Classified documents, if they indeed exist, remain hidden from public view, leaving a void filled with speculation and conspiracy theories. The potential intersection of government interests with the deeply personal experiences of abductees raises ethical questions about the role of secrecy in the pursuit of knowledge.

Psychologically, the impact of alien abduction experiences extends beyond the realm of the tangible and enters the territory of the subconscious. Reports of missing time, repressed memories, and the sensation of being under the control of external forces create a labyrinth of psychological challenges for those who claim to have undergone abduction. The blurred line between reality and perceived reality adds a layer of complexity to the analysis of these encounters, inviting speculation about the interplay of memory, trauma, and the unknown.

Speculation also extends to the motivations behind potential government involvement in studying or concealing alien abduction phenomena. Theories range from the altruistic—seeking to protect public safety and prevent mass hysteria—to the more sinister—exploiting advanced extraterrestrial technologies for military or covert purposes. The intersection of personal narratives with classified information introduces a narrative tension between individual experiences and the broader context of government secrecy, leaving us to navigate the enigmatic landscapes of both subjective reality and potential covert operations.

Here we will look at and bring to life some of the most bizarre and mysterious personal narratives and classified information and see how where the intertwine. The psychological and emotional dimensions of these experiences create a complex tapestry that challenges our understanding of the unknown. As we navigate the intersection of public disclosures and potential government involvement, we find ourselves in a realm where the deeply personal stories of abductees coalesce with the elusive shadows of classified information, inviting us to contemplate the profound mysteries embedded within the abduction phenomenon.

Within the vast landscape of alien abduction literature, personal accounts often delve into chilling details, including the perplexing phenomena of lost time and unexplained marks on abductees' bodies. These narratives, while diverse in their specifics, share common threads that fuel speculation and intrigue. As we continue to unravel these accounts, we navigate the intricacies of missing time and mysterious markings, venturing into the speculative realms that seek to make sense of these enigmatic experiences.

Lost Time:

A recurrent theme in abduction accounts is the unsettling sensation of missing time—an unexplained gap in an individual's memory during the alleged abduction event. Abductees often report a sense of disorientation, realizing that hours have passed without any recollection of the events that transpired.

The nature of this temporal distortion transcends conventional explanations, leading to speculation about the manipulation of human perception or the possibility of extradimensional experiences.

Speculation surrounds the idea that the manipulation of time might be a deliberate aspect of extraterrestrial encounters. Theories posit that advanced beings could possess the capability to alter human perception, creating temporal anomalies that serve both to facilitate their activities and to confound human understanding. The subjective experience of lost time adds a psychological layer to abduction accounts, challenging abductees to grapple with the elusive nature of the encounters and the malleability of their own perceptions.

Unusual Marks:

Another intriguing facet of abduction accounts involves the discovery of unusual marks on the bodies of those who claim to have been abducted. These marks often take the form of scars, bruises, or puncture wounds, and their origin remains a subject of speculation. Abductees recount waking up with unexplained injuries, sometimes in specific patterns or arrangements, sparking theories about the purpose and origin of these marks.

Speculative avenues explore the possibility that these marks serve as physical evidence of extraterrestrial examinations or procedures. Some theories suggest that these marks could be the result of medical examinations conducted by advanced beings, possibly involving the collection of genetic material or the implantation of tracking devices. The enigmatic nature of these markings adds an unsettling layer to abduction narratives, raising questions about the nature of the purported interactions between abductees and their alleged extraterrestrial abductors.

The speculative landscape surrounding lost time and unusual marks is vast, encompassing a spectrum of possibilities that range from psychological explanations to considerations of advanced extraterrestrial technologies. Some theories propose that the altered states of consciousness experienced during abductions might contribute to the perception of lost time, suggesting a connection between the mind and the temporal distortions reported by abductees.

In the realm of unusual marks, speculative theories extend to the potential use of advanced medical technologies by extraterrestrial beings. The idea that these marks represent evidence of medical examinations or experiments forms a narrative thread that weaves through abduction literature. The possibility that these procedures serve a specific purpose, such as genetic study or monitoring, fuels discussions about the intentions and motivations behind the alleged abductions.

The exploration of personal accounts detailing lost time and unusual marks immerses us in the complex and enigmatic world of alien abductions. The convergence of subjective experiences, temporal distortions, and unexplained physical markings invites us to navigate the speculative landscapes that seek to unravel the mysteries embedded within these narratives. As we delve into the possibilities and speculations surrounding these accounts, we confront the profound implications that the intersection of the unknown and the deeply personal holds for our understanding of the cosmos and the nature of human-alien interactions.

We can't help but be fascinated by the intriguing realm of atomic-level engineering and its potential connection to extraterrestrial influence. As our understanding of physics and engineering progresses, whispers of technologies beyond our current capabilities have surfaced. By examining declassified information and scientific speculations, we explore the possibility that classified research projects are venturing into realms of knowledge inspired by encounters with extraterrestrial intelligence. Within this deep dive, we navigate the landscape of public opinion, considering the implications and speculations surrounding atomic-level engineering and its potential extraterrestrial influences.

Declassified Information:

In deeply analyzing and examining recently declassified information, tantalizing glimpses of advanced technologies emerge, sparking speculation about atomic-level engineering inspired by encounters with extraterrestrial entities. Reports hint at classified research projects exploring propulsion systems, materials science, and engineering principles that seem to defy conventional understanding. These whispers provide a narrative backdrop that invites us to contemplate the existence of a hidden realm of scientific knowledge, potentially influenced by interactions with extraterrestrial intelligence.

Public opinion becomes a dynamic canvas upon which the brushstrokes of speculation and skepticism create a nuanced portrait of atomic-level engineering with potential extraterrestrial origins. While some embrace the notion of scientific advancements driven by encounters with extraterrestrial entities, others approach such ideas with skepticism, attributing advanced technologies to terrestrial ingenuity rather than extraterrestrial influence. The interplay of belief systems, scientific curiosity, and skepticism within the public sphere adds layers of complexity to the discourse surrounding atomic-level engineering.

Technological Implications:

The exploration of atomic-level engineering raises profound questions about the potential technological implications of extraterrestrial influence. Speculations extend to propulsion systems that operate on principles beyond our current understanding of physics, materials with unprecedented properties, and engineering feats that seemingly defy the limits of terrestrial knowledge. The fusion of scientific advancements with potential extraterrestrial insights becomes a narrative thread that weaves through discussions about the future trajectory of human technological progress.

Scientific speculations surrounding atomic-level engineering explore the boundaries of known physics and materials science. The prospect of technologies inspired by extraterrestrial intelligence raises questions about the nature of scientific inquiry and the possibilities that may lie beyond our current understanding. Theoretical frameworks involving advancements in quantum mechanics, exotic materials, and novel engineering principles become part of the speculative discourse, inviting us to contemplate the potential intersections between terrestrial and extraterrestrial knowledge.

The potential reality of atomic-level engineering influenced by extraterrestrial encounters carries implications for society at large. The prospect of revolutionary technologies capable of transforming industries, energy systems, and transportation introduces both excitement and apprehension. The societal impact of such advancements, whether driven by human ingenuity or extraterrestrial inspiration, becomes a focal point of discussions about the ethical, economic, and geopolitical consequences of unlocking the secrets of atomic-level engineering.

Cultural Narratives:

Cultural narratives surrounding atomic-level engineering and extraterrestrial influence weave a tapestry that reflects societal attitudes, fears, and aspirations. Science fiction and popular media contribute to shaping public perceptions of what might be possible, blurring the lines between speculative fiction and potential scientific realities. The cultural imagination becomes a crucible where ideas about the fusion of extraterrestrial insights with human technological prowess are molded, influencing how society envisions the future of scientific and engineering achievements.

This invites us to explore the realm of atomic-level engineering and its potential connection to extraterrestrial influence. The interplay between declassified information, public opinion, technological implications, scientific speculations, impacts on society, and cultural narratives forms a multidimensional narrative that challenges our understanding of the boundaries of scientific knowledge. As we navigate this terrain, we confront the tantalizing possibility that encounters with extraterrestrial intelligence might be leaving an indelible mark on the forefront of human technological progress, opening doors to realms of knowledge that transcend the limits of our current understanding.

The clandestine nature surrounding advanced technologies, particularly those tied to atomic-level engineering with potential extraterrestrial influence, prompts a deep dive into the motivations behind their secrecy and the multifaceted implications for modern warfare, technological advancement, and our exploration of the cosmos.

Secrecy and National Security:

One of the primary reasons for keeping advanced technologies under wraps is rooted in national security concerns. Governments may withhold information to maintain a strategic advantage over potential adversaries. Technologies derived from atomic-level engineering, influenced by encounters with extraterrestrial intelligence, could provide a significant edge in warfare, prompting the need for secrecy to protect these advantages.

The potential applications of advanced technologies in modern warfare are vast and transformative. Propulsion systems capable of defying known physics, materials with unprecedented strength or adaptability, and weaponry that operates on exotic principles could reshape the battlefield. Secrecy becomes a tool not only to protect these advancements but also to utilize them strategically, avoiding premature disclosure that might erode their effectiveness.

Advancement of Human Understanding on Weaponry:

The study of atomic-level engineering influenced by extraterrestrial encounters could propel human understanding of weaponry to unprecedented levels. Insights into exotic materials, energy sources, and propulsion systems may revolutionize the development of weapons with capabilities far beyond current understanding. Secrecy in this context serves as a means to control the narrative, ensuring that these advancements are exploited strategically and responsibly.

Cosmic Exploration and Technological Leapfrogging:

Extraterrestrial influence on atomic-level engineering may not be limited to military applications. The technology derived from such encounters could catalyze a leap in our ability to explore the cosmos. Advanced propulsion systems could revolutionize space travel, potentially unlocking the means to reach distant celestial bodies more efficiently. The secrecy surrounding these technologies becomes a means to harness their potential for exploration while guarding against misuse.

Technological Advantages in a Global Context:

In a global context, possession of advanced technologies derived from atomic-level engineering offers geopolitical advantages. Nations with access to these technologies can assert dominance in various spheres, influencing economic, diplomatic, and scientific landscapes. The strategic withholding of information ensures a competitive edge, fostering a technological arms race that shapes the global power dynamic.

The secrecy surrounding advanced technologies also raises ethical considerations. The potential for misuse or unintended consequences necessitates a careful balance between technological advancement and responsible use. Governments must weigh the benefits of maintaining a strategic edge against the risks associated with the uncontrolled proliferation of technologies that could reshape the very fabric of our existence.

Humanity's Technological Trajectory:

The exploration of atomic-level engineering, inspired by extraterrestrial encounters, reflects humanity's ongoing trajectory of technological evolution. Secrecy becomes intertwined with the responsibility to guide this evolution, ensuring that advancements are integrated into society in a manner that benefits humanity without compromising its values, security, or ethical principles.

the deep dive into the secrecy surrounding advanced technologies derived from atomic-level engineering, potentially influenced by extraterrestrial encounters, reveals a complex interplay of national security, advancements in warfare, cosmic exploration, and global power dynamics. The implications extend beyond the confines of Earth, shaping the trajectory of human technological evolution and raising critical ethical considerations. As we navigate this intricate landscape, we confront the delicate balance between secrecy, responsible use, and the potential for transformative advancements that could redefine our understanding of both the cosmos and the nature of technological progress.

Chapter 9: Moon Mysteries and Enigmatic Bases: Unraveling Cosmic Intrigues

The corridors of conspiracy theories is the idea of extraterrestrial bases on the moon. From clandestine lunar landings to convert extraterrestrial collaborations, accounts have surfaced suggesting that the moon serves as a hub for extraterrestrial civilizations. Whistleblowers and self-proclaimed insiders have shared tales of secret lunar installations, sparking debates about the existence of structures hidden beneath the lunar surface.

Mysterious lights and unexplained phenomena observed on the moon have fueled speculation about the presence of extraterrestrial intelligence. Anecdotes from astronomers and lunar observers describe unexplained flashes, transient lights, and unusual activities on the lunar surface. While skeptics attribute these phenomena to natural causes, proponents of lunar mysteries argue that they may be signals, beacons, or evidence of technological activity beyond our understanding.

The accounts surrounding lunar mysteries weave a complex narrative that spans extraterrestrial bases, mysterious lights, and terrestrial connections. As we navigate the cosmic landscape of speculation and exploration, the moon remains an enigmatic protagonist, a celestial companion that has witnessed the ebb and flow of human fascination. Whether these accounts align with scientific understanding or reside in the realms of conspiracy, the cosmic quest persists, beckoning humanity to gaze skyward and contemplate the mysteries that linger in the lunar shadows.

In the celestial tapestry that graces our night skies, the moon, Earth's silent companion, stands as a luminescent enigma, invoking tales of extraterrestrial mysteries and concealed structures. As whispers of lunar bases and unexplained lights echo through the cosmic corridors, a captivating journey into the realms of speculation and exploration unfolds, inviting us to unravel the secrets that the moon guards with an inscrutable glow.

Extraterrestrial Bases: Bridging Earth and Moon

The notion of extraterrestrial bases on the moon has tantalized the curious and sparked the imaginations of those drawn to the cosmic unknown. Accounts of clandestine installations beneath the lunar surface, hidden from the prying eyes of terrestrial observers, have permeated conspiracy theories. Whistleblowers and purported insiders weave narratives of cosmic collaborations, suggesting that the moon serves as a rendezvous point for extraterrestrial intelligences. Yet, as we embark on this cosmic deep dive, it is imperative to tread the delicate balance between speculative intrigue and empirical evidence.

Astronauts, Astronomers, and lunar observers recount tales of fleeting lights, momentary flashes, and anomalies that defy conventional explanations. Are these merely cosmic aberrations, manifestations of natural processes, or do they signify a more profound cosmic communication? The shadows cast by lunar mysteries extend beyond the realms of scientific inquiry, beckoning us to contemplate the cosmic ballet with an open mind.

Antarctica's Cosmic Connection: Where Earth Meets Moon

The allure of lunar mysteries extends beyond the cosmic ballet, drawing connections to Earth's southernmost continent—Antarctica. Within the lore of conspiracy theories, tales of secret lunar bases find terrestrial counterparts beneath the icy expanses of Antarctica. A speculative narrative unfolds, intertwining the moon's mysteries with hidden structures buried beneath the polar ice. While grounded in intrigue, these accounts push the boundaries of plausibility, prompting us to navigate a delicate cosmic dance between fact and fiction.

Underwater Bases: A Submerged Cosmic Odyssey

As the cosmic voyage unfolds, whispers emerge of extraterrestrial bases not only in celestial realms but beneath the Earth's oceans. Submerged structures hidden in the depths become part of a cosmic narrative that bridges the lunar enigmas with Earth's unexplored aquatic realms. The concept of underwater cosmic gateways introduces a surreal dimension to the mysteries, blurring the boundaries between speculative tales and the uncharted realities of Earth's watery expanses.

In the cosmic labyrinth of lunar mysteries, discerning truth from speculation becomes an intricate journey. While some narratives align with scientific scrutiny and a genuine quest for understanding, others border on the fantastical, weaving tales of cosmic collaboration and covert activities. As we venture deeper into this cosmic odyssey, it is essential to acknowledge the nuanced dance between imagination and empirical evidence, recognizing that the truth may reside in the delicate interplay of both.

The moon remains an enigmatic celestial companion that has inspired tales of extraterrestrial bases and cosmic connections with Earth's distant landscapes. Whether rooted in scientific inquiry or nurtured by the fertile grounds of conspiracy theories, the cosmic quest persists. The moon, veiled in its luminescent mystery, continues to beckon us into the celestial unknown, where the line between speculation and truth becomes as elusive as the cosmic lights that dance upon its surface. As we explore the cosmic waters of lunar mysteries, the journey unfolds not merely as an exploration of extraterrestrial possibilities but as an invitation to contemplate the enduring allure of the cosmic unknown that stretches beyond the confines of our terrestrial understanding.

Chapter 10: International Collaboration on UFO Research

Investigate how the declassification and sharing of UFO information have led to international collaboration on research and investigations. Explore the potential benefits and challenges of countries working together to understand these phenomena.

The declassification and sharing of UFO information have triggered a paradigm shift, fostering international collaboration on research and investigations into these mysterious phenomena. As countries open their vaults of classified information, the global community is presented with an opportunity to collectively unravel the enigma of unidentified aerial phenomena (UAP). In this deep dive, we explore how this collaboration has unfolded, examining the potential benefits and challenges that arise when nations join forces to comprehend the mysteries that linger in our skies.

Decades of secrecy surrounding UFO-related information have seen a gradual shift as governments release classified documents. Initiatives to declassify UFO information, driven by a growing public interest and changing attitudes, have occurred in various countries. The United States, in particular, has taken steps to disclose information through programs like the Advanced Aerospace Threat Identification Program (AATIP). As information becomes more accessible, the stage is set for international collaboration.

The sharing of declassified UFO information has paved the way for international collaboration in research and investigations. Countries with a history of UFO encounters, such as the United States, Russia, and several European nations, are now more inclined to cooperate in understanding the nature of these phenomena. Collaborative research efforts involve sharing data, conducting joint studies, and establishing frameworks for coordinated investigations.

1. Data Corroboration: International collaboration allows for the corroboration of UFO sightings and encounters. By pooling data from different regions, researchers can identify patterns, trends, or anomalies that may not be apparent when examining isolated incidents. This strengthens the scientific foundation for understanding UAP.

2. Diverse Perspectives: Collaboration brings together diverse scientific, cultural, and technological perspectives. Different nations may possess unique analytical tools, expertise, and approaches to investigating UAP. This diversity enhances the comprehensiveness of research efforts, fostering a more holistic understanding.

3. Resource Sharing: Collaborative efforts enable the sharing of resources, both technical and financial. Jointly funded research projects and shared access to advanced technologies can accelerate progress in studying UAP, mitigating the limitations that individual nations might face in isolation.

4. Enhanced Credibility: International collaboration lends credibility to UFO research. When multiple countries affirm the importance of understanding these phenomena, it elevates the scientific discourse surrounding UAP, potentially reducing skepticism and stigma associated with the topic.

Challenges and Considerations:

1. Security Concerns: Sharing sensitive information related to national security may pose challenges. Countries may be hesitant to disclose certain details, especially if UFO encounters involve military

operations or technologies. Striking a balance between transparency and security becomes crucial.

2. Cultural Differences: Collaborating nations may have different cultural perspectives on UFO phenomena. Variances in public attitudes, religious beliefs, and cultural interpretations of extraterrestrial encounters can influence the direction and acceptance of collaborative research.

3. Political Sensitivities: The political climate can impact collaboration. UFO research may be subject to political agendas or diplomatic considerations. Striking a balance between scientific inquiry and political sensitivities requires careful navigation.

4. Technological Disparities: Not all countries possess the same technological capabilities for researching UAP. Disparities in equipment, expertise, and infrastructure may affect the level of contribution each nation can make to collaborative efforts.

Close Encounters of the Fifth Kind: Bridging the Cosmic Chasm

In the lexicon of extraterrestrial encounters, the notion of Close Encounters of the Fifth Kind (CE5) stands as a beacon illuminating the potential for direct communication between humans and extraterrestrial entities. Beyond mere sightings, CE5 ventures into the realm of intentional human-initiated contact, sparking a tapestry of public speculation, mystery, and the quest for meaning in the cosmic expanse.

Defining the Close Encounter: Levels of Cosmic Interaction

Close Encounters, as popularized by the work of ufologist J. Allen Hynek, are classified into different levels, with the Fifth Kind representing the pinnacle of intentional human-initiated contact. CE5 involves conscious efforts by individuals or groups to establish communication with extraterrestrial intelligences through methods such as meditation, visualization, or other forms of telepathic outreach. The intentional nature of these encounters transforms the cosmic narrative from passive observers to active participants.

Public Speculation: From Skepticism to Enthusiasm

Public reactions to the concept of CE5 span a spectrum of skepticism, intrigue, and enthusiastic belief. Skeptics often view the idea of intentional contact with extraterrestrial beings as fanciful, attributing sightings and experiences to psychological phenomena or misinterpretations of natural occurrences. Conversely, enthusiasts embrace the notion that humanity possesses the agency to reach out to cosmic neighbors, viewing CE5 as a transformative and spiritually enlightening endeavor.

Mystery Shrouded in Conscious Intent: The CE5 Experience

The essence of CE5 lies not only in the reported encounters but in the deliberate actions taken by individuals to initiate contact. Practitioners describe entering meditative states, employing visualization techniques, or utilizing consciousness-altering methods to establish a connection with extraterrestrial entities. The mystery lies not only in the reported sightings or telepathic exchanges but in the inherent challenge of verifying and understanding these experiences.

Symbolism and Symbolic Communication: Decoding the Cosmic Lexicon

CE5 experiences often involve symbolic communication, where individuals report receiving messages or impressions conveyed through symbols, images, or thoughts. Decoding this cosmic lexicon becomes a herculean task, as symbols may carry personal significance or universal archetypes. The challenge lies in discerning whether these symbols represent genuine communication from extraterrestrial intelligences or are projections of the human psyche onto the cosmic canvas.

The Search for Meaning: Bridging the Cosmic Chasm

As practitioners engage in intentional contact through CE5, the quest for meaning becomes a central motif. Whether seeking spiritual enlightenment, cosmic unity, or answers to existential questions, those who embark on the journey to bridge the cosmic chasm through direct interaction grapple with the profound implications of human-initiated contact. The search for meaning extends beyond the stars, transcending the boundaries of scientific scrutiny and delving into the realms of metaphysics and consciousness exploration.

Conclusion: CE5 as a Cosmic Frontier

In the cosmic tapestry of extraterrestrial encounters, Close Encounters of the Fifth Kind emerge as a cosmic frontier where human consciousness reaches out to touch the unknown. Public speculation surrounding CE5 reflects the diverse perspectives that humanity holds toward the possibility of intentional contact with extraterrestrial intelligences. The mysteries enshrouded in conscious intent, symbolic communication, and the search for meaning beckon us to explore the uncharted territories of the cosmic psyche, challenging us to transcend the limitations of our understanding and reach for the stars with the hopeful expectation that, just perhaps, the cosmos may respond in kind.

International collaboration on UFO research transcends individual nations and holds broader implications for humanity. The study of UAP represents a shared endeavor that extends beyond geopolitical boundaries. As nations collaborate to unravel the mysteries of the cosmos, the global community becomes more interconnected in its pursuit of knowledge and understanding.

Surveillance in the Shadows: Advanced Technologies and the Nuclear Enigma

In the ever-evolving landscape of technological prowess, a question looms large over the collective consciousness: are we being watched? This deep dive plunges into the realms of advanced technologies, their potential implications for humanity, and the enigmatic interference that shadows nuclear missions, shrouding them in a cloak of mystery. As we navigate this intricate cosmic dance between surveillance, technological prowess, and the nuclear unknown, we unveil a tapestry woven with threads of speculation, intrigue, and the perennial quest for understanding.

Advanced Technologies: Guardians or Intruders?

The exponential rise of advanced technologies has ushered humanity into an era where surveillance capabilities reach unprecedented heights. From ubiquitous satellites and drones to cutting-edge artificial intelligence, the watchful eye of technology extends across the globe. The seamless integration of surveillance systems into everyday life sparks a nuanced dialogue about the balance between security and privacy, raising concerns about the boundaries that define the ever-watchful gaze of modern technologies.

Nuclear Power: A Double-Edged Sword

In the realm of energy and scientific innovation, nuclear power stands as a symbol of both promise and peril. The potential for clean, efficient energy is juxtaposed with the ominous specter of nuclear weapons, casting a shadow over the peaceful applications of atomic energy. As nations harness the power of the atom for electricity generation, questions arise about the safeguards in place to prevent the malevolent use of nuclear technologies and the ethical considerations surrounding their deployment.

The Nuclear Enigma: Interference and Shadows

As humanity ventures further into the cosmic unknown, the enigma of interference in nuclear missions emerges as a cryptic subplot. Whispers of unexplained phenomena, unidentified flying objects, and uncharted anomalies surround nuclear facilities, creating a cosmic canvas where terrestrial and extraterrestrial forces converge. Reports of inexplicable disruptions in missile systems and untraceable interference raise questions about the potential cosmic spectators, monitoring humanity's atomic endeavors with an inscrutable gaze.

Mystery in the Silos: Unraveling Nuclear Anomalies

Within the confines of nuclear silos and military installations, tales of unidentified intrusions weave a narrative that blurs the lines between the known and the unknown. Incidents where nuclear missiles inexplicably malfunction or encounter unexplained interference fuel speculation about the involvement of advanced extraterrestrial technologies. The cosmic mystery embedded within these anomalies challenges our understanding of the limits of human technological control and invites us to contemplate the cosmic forces that may silently observe our nuclear pursuits.

In contemplating the intricate dance of surveillance, advanced technologies, and the nuclear enigma, the delicate balance between vigilance and secrecy becomes a central theme. While surveillance technologies serve as guardians against potential threats, they also raise concerns about the erosion of personal privacy and the potential for abuse. In the realm of nuclear activities, the fine line between transparency and the need for classified information emerges as a complex challenge, prompting a nuanced discussion about the ethical and security implications of the nuclear unknown.

As we navigate the cosmic watchtower of advanced technologies and the nuclear enigma, the journey unfolds as a tapestry woven with threads of complexity, uncertainty, and the perpetual quest for understanding. The gaze of surveillance technologies, both terrestrial and potentially extraterrestrial, challenges humanity to navigate the delicate balance between security and privacy.

The cosmic shadows that cast their silhouette over nuclear missions invite us to contemplate the cosmic forces that may silently observe our endeavors, raising profound questions about the interconnectedness of our technological pursuits with the enigmatic cosmic unknown. In this cosmic dance, the quest for understanding persists, urging humanity to tread the delicate path between illumination and the shadows that linger in the realms of advanced technologies and the nuclear enigma.

The declassification and sharing of UFO information have catalyzed international collaboration on research and investigations. The benefits of data corroboration, diverse perspectives, resource sharing, and enhanced credibility are countered by challenges related to security concerns, cultural differences, political sensitivities, and technological disparities. As nations collectively probe the mysteries of unidentified aerial phenomena, the collaborative efforts unfold on a global stage, shaping the trajectory of our understanding of the cosmos and fostering a sense of shared responsibility in exploring the enigmas that linger above.

The exploration of UFOs, UAP, and whistleblower accounts converges upon a nexus of possibilities, challenges, and the perpetual quest for understanding. The declassification of information, emergence of public awareness, and burgeoning international cooperation mark a transformative juncture in our collective engagement with the cosmic unknown.

The act of declassifying UFO information signifies not only a shift in governmental transparency but also an acknowledgment of the public's right to explore the mysteries that linger in our skies. As the veils of secrecy are lifted, a new era of awareness dawns, prompting a global dialogue that transcends borders and cultures. The public, armed with information, becomes an active participant in the discourse surrounding unidentified aerial phenomena, challenging established narratives and catalyzing a reevaluation of our place in the cosmos.

International cooperation in UFO research heralds a paradigm where nations set aside geopolitical differences to collectively fathom the enigmas that transcend terrestrial boundaries. Collaboration offers the promise of a richer tapestry of knowledge, as diverse perspectives and resources converge to unravel the intricacies of cosmic phenomena. Yet, within this alliance lies the challenge of navigating political sensitivities, security concerns, and the intricacies of intercultural collaboration, urging us to tread carefully as we navigate the global pursuit of cosmic comprehension.

The speculative horizon stretches before us, beckoning us to contemplate the potential benefits and dangers implicated in our evolving understanding of UFO phenomena. From technological advancements that could redefine our capabilities to the ethical considerations of wielding newfound knowledge, the future holds both promise and peril. The fusion of scientific inquiry, public engagement, and international collaboration propels us into uncharted territories, where the mysteries of the cosmos become a shared canvas for exploration.

As we stand on the precipice of an era defined by declassification, public awareness, and international cooperation, the journey into the cosmic unknown unfolds. The potential benefits extend beyond scientific discoveries, touching upon cultural evolution, technological innovation, and the forging of a collective human narrative that stretches into the cosmic realms. Yet, with these opportunities come responsibilities—to navigate the uncertainties with wisdom, to safeguard against misuse, and to embrace the unknown with a reverence for the mysteries that defy our current understanding.

In our cosmic exploration, let us move forward with open minds, fostering a spirit of collaboration, and acknowledging that the pursuit of truth is a dynamic voyage rather than a static destination. The unfolding future invites us to become stewards of knowledge, guardians of ethical inquiry, and partners in the cosmic dance that beckons us ever onward into the unexplored realms of the celestial unknown.

Epilogue: Beyond the Horizon of Mystery

As we reach the concluding pages of this cosmic exploration, it is essential to acknowledge the enduring essence of mystery that remains intertwined with the fabric of our existence. Despite the strides we have taken in unraveling the secrets of the cosmos, the vast expanse still echoes with enigmas that elude our understanding—a reminder that the universe, in its unfathomable complexity, continues to hold secrets beyond the grasp of our current comprehension.

Mystery, in its essence, is the uncharted terrain where knowledge meets humility, where the known converges with the unknown. It is the cosmic canvas upon which our insatiable curiosity paints the tapestry of discovery, each revelation leading us to new questions, new frontiers, and new realms of wonder. The allure of mystery is not a testament to our limitations but an invitation to embark on an eternal quest for understanding.

The historical path we have threaded, from the first steps on the moon to the exploration of distant planets, reflects the indomitable spirit of human curiosity. Technological advancements have propelled us forward, unveiling the cosmic theater in unprecedented detail. Our journey has been a testament to the symbiotic dance between innovation and the relentless pursuit of knowledge, a journey that echoes the collective heartbeat of a species poised on the brink of cosmic enlightenment.

As we stand on the precipice of a future teeming with promises of warp drive technology, mastery of gravity manipulation, and the harnessing of nuclear energy for celestial propulsion, we glimpse the contours of a new era. The speculative horizons beckon us toward a cosmic frontier where the boundaries of what we once deemed impossible dissolve into the luminous tapestry of the conceivable. The future holds the promise of transcending the limitations of our current understanding, a future where humanity may navigate the cosmic currents with newfound dexterity.

In this realm of speculation, where the dreams of warp drives and gravity manipulation become the harbinger of potential realities, we find ourselves at a juncture where science fiction and scientific inquiry converge. The line between the speculative and the achievable blurs, inviting us to ponder the profound implications of a future where the cosmic unknown becomes not just a destination but a canvas for the masterpieces of human innovation.

This cosmic odyssey is not an endpoint but a waypoint—a moment to reflect on the mysteries we have unraveled, the questions that linger, and the boundless potential that awaits us. The journey into the cosmic unknown is a perpetual voyage, and as we turn the page into the unwritten chapters of tomorrow, may the spirit of inquiry, the pursuit of knowledge, and the thrill of discovery guide us into a future where the cosmos, in all its mystery, becomes a shared sanctuary of understanding for generations yet to come.

Are We Alone in the Universe? Unraveling the Mysteries of UFOs and UAPs

The age-old question of whether we are alone in the vast cosmic expanse has lingered in the corridors of human contemplation for centuries. As sightings of Unidentified Flying Objects (UFOs) and Unidentified Aerial Phenomena (UAPs) persist, the notion that extraterrestrial life may not only exist but has traversed the incomprehensible distances of the universe to visit Earth sparks a profound exploration into the mysteries that dance on the edge of our understanding.

The quest to answer the question of extraterrestrial life extends beyond the realms of scientific inquiry into the fabric of human curiosity. The universe, with its billions of galaxies and trillions of stars, presents a canvas that hints at the possibility of life beyond our pale blue dot. As technology advances, our ability to peer into the cosmic tapestry deepens, revealing the potential habitable zones and exoplanets that may host life as we know it. Yet, the elusive nature of extraterrestrial intelligence remains one of the greatest enigmas of our cosmic odyssey.

Advanced Technology: Beyond the Bounds of Earthly Understanding

If extraterrestrial life has indeed journeyed to Earth, their technology must surpass our current understanding of aviation and propulsion systems. The sightings of UFOs and UAPs often depict movements and maneuvers that defy the laws of physics as we comprehend them. Accelerations, decelerations, and sudden changes in direction challenge the very principles of aerodynamics. The question arises: What technology could propel a craft across the vastness of space and navigate our atmosphere with such apparent ease? The mystery lies not only in their existence but in the technological marvels that accompany their presence.

Fear of the Unknown: Speculation and Misinterpretation

The mysteries surrounding UFOs and UAPs often evoke a sense of fear and trepidation. The unknown, with its cloak of uncertainty, has the power to elicit apprehension about the intentions and motivations behind these celestial visitors. The human psyche, prone to fear of the unfamiliar, grapples with the uncertainties that shroud these extraterrestrial encounters. The narratives of government cover-ups and classified operations add a layer of suspicion, blurring the line between what is concealed for national security and what may be hidden about potential extraterrestrial interactions.

Technological Marvels or Classified Options?

In the quest for truth, the possibility that these unidentified phenomena may be classified human-made technologies cannot be dismissed. Stealth aircraft, experimental drones, or other top-secret projects could account for some sightings. However, the sheer scale and magnitude of certain events challenge the notion that all encounters can be explained away as terrestrial experiments. The distinct possibility remains that a portion of these sightings may indeed be beyond the purview of our earthly technological advancements.

Speculation and Seeking the Truth: The Human Imperative

The inability to definitively answer the question of extraterrestrial life and the mysteries surrounding

UFOs and UAPs compels humanity to speculate and seek the truth. The pursuit of knowledge, fueled by our innate curiosity, motivates scientists, researchers, and enthusiasts to unravel the cosmic riddles that dance on the edges of our understanding. The cosmic ballet of lights in the night sky beckons us to explore the unknown, to transcend the limitations of our current scientific paradigms, and to embrace the possibility that we may not be alone in the universe.

In conclusion, the question of whether we are alone in the universe and the mysteries of UFOs and UAPs weave a tapestry that encompasses the realms of science, speculation, and the human quest for knowledge. The technology displayed by these unidentified phenomena challenges our understanding, while the fear of the unknown adds layers of complexity to the narrative. As humanity continues to gaze skyward and peer into the cosmic unknown, the mysteries that unfold above may hold the keys to understanding not only our place in the universe but the potential existence of other intelligences navigating the vast cosmic sea.

Sources and Recommended Reading, Articles and Publications

1. "Cosmic Chronicles: Unveiling the Secrets of the Universe"
2. "Beyond the Horizon: Exploring Cosmic Mysteries"

3. "Celestial Enigma: Journeys into Unknown Realms"

4. "Galactic Whispers: Stories from the Cosmic Tapestry"

5. "Stellar Odyssey: Navigating the Cosmos of Discovery"

6. "Mysteries of the Cosmos: Tales from the Galactic Unknown"

7. "Eclipsing the Unknown: Adventures in Cosmic Inquiry"

8. "Warping Horizons: A Cosmic Quest for Understanding"

9. "Cosmic Conundrums: A Journey through Uncharted Realms"

10. "Infinite Echoes: Cosmic Wonders and Enigmatic Tales"

11. "Beyond Earth: Chronicles of Cosmic Exploration"

12. "Spectral Voyages: Unraveling the Veil of Cosmic Secrets"

13. "Starlight Chronicles: Probing the Depths of Cosmic Mysteries"

14. "Luminary Whispers: Revelations from the Cosmic Ether"

15. "Interstellar Intrigues: Uncharted Territories of the Universe"

16. "Astral Revelations: Navigating the Cosmos of Wonder"

17. "Celestial Riddles: Unlocking the Secrets of the Stars"

18. "Quantum Quest: Cosmic Puzzles and Infinite Possibilities"

19. "Chronicles of the Cosmos: Tales of Cosmic Inquiry"

20. "Exploring Infinity: Cosmic Tales of Discovery and Wonder"

21. "Secrets of the S Nevada Sky: The Area 51 Enigma Unveiled"

22. "Lazar's Revelation: A Glimpse Inside the Alien Archives"

23. "Area 51 Chronicles: Decoding Extraterrestrial Whispers"

24. "Bob Lazar's Legacy: UFOs, Reverse Engineering, and Truths Unearthed"

25. "Eyes on the Skies: Area 51 and the Quest for Extraterrestrial Knowledge"

26. "Behind the Perimeter: Uncovering Area 51's Hidden Realms"

27. "Bob Lazar: From Area 51 to Cosmic Secrets"

28. "Area 51 Unmasked: The De-classified UFO Files Exposed"

29. "Lazar's Odyssey: A Journey into the Unknown"

30. "Cosmic Controversies: Area 51, Bob Lazar, and the UFO Phenomena"

31. "Secrets in the Desert: The Mystique of Area 51 Revealed"

32. "Whispers from the Black Vault: Bob Lazar's Untold Stories"

33. "Area 51 Chronicles: A Close Encounter with the Unknown"

34. "Lazar's Legacy: UFOs, Government Secrets, and the Road to Disclosure"

35. "Decoding the Desert: Area 51's Extraterrestrial Conundrums"

36. "Bob Lazar Unveiled: UFOs, Alien Technology, and the Quest for Truth"

37. "Area 51 Alchemy: Bob Lazar's Revelations and Beyond"

38. "UFO Confessions: Inside Area 51 and the Revelations of Bob Lazar"

39. "Eclipsing Secrets: The Enigma of Area 51 and Bob Lazar's Testimony"

40. "Lazar's Disclosure: Unraveling the Extraterrestrial Mysteries of Area 51"

Made in the USA
Las Vegas, NV
28 May 2024

90474495R00105